The Whole Counsel of GOD

An Introduction to Your Bible

REV. DR. STEPHEN DE YOUNG

ANCIENT FAITH PUBLISHING
CHESTERTON, INDIANA

The Whole Counsel of God: An Introduction to Your Bible
Copyright ©2022 Stephen De Young

Published by:
Ancient Faith Publishing
A Division of Ancient Faith Ministries
1050 Broadway, Suite 6
Chesterton, IN 46304

Cover images: leather background, donatas1205/Shutterstock; icon of Christ Pantocrator, zatletic-stock.adobe.com

ISBN: 978-1-955890-19-9

Library of Congress Control Number: 2022937551

Contents

Introduction

A S MODERN PEOPLE, WE ARE used to thinking of the Bible as a printed book. If we are Christians, we likely have the idea that we ought to read it. This usually takes the form of feeling guilty that we don't read it more often than we do. We have been taught that answers to life's most difficult questions are contained within it, and, by reading it, we will draw closer to Christ and become better people. But attempt to read the Bible cover to cover and you'll likely run out of steam somewhere between the extended descriptions of sacrificial rituals and the laws governing cleansing a home of mildew. Opening to a random page might produce a nugget of truth that we can chew on for the rest of our lives, or it might inform us that "Uz was the brother of Buz" in the midst of a long genealogy of unpronounceable names.

The Bible has also become a rhetorical tool in our public discourse. On moral issues that touch on present-day political controversies, non-Christian commentators frequently refer to the Bible as saying this or that. We are told, for example, that the Bible says a woman who has been raped must marry her rapist. Or that God ordered Israel to commit genocide against innocent Canaanite women and children. When a Christian commentator refers to the Bible as an authority on sexual morality, on the other hand, the response is often that the Christian is a hypocrite, because the Bible also says that it is wrong to eat shellfish or wear a blend of two fabrics. On both sides, those who make these statements would be hard pressed, if handed a Bible, to find exactly where it says these things. Nevertheless, people hear such claims about the Bible and internalize them.

Within the Christian world, dozens of Protestant groups likewise make a dizzying array of claims as to what exactly the Bible teaches. They declare that their beliefs and the very organization of their communities are biblical. But these groups also disagree about theology, and their communities are organized differently. Other Protestants will cast doubt on whether the Bible actually teaches anything. They embrace the subjectivity of biblical interpretation and so will talk about various interpretive options and perspectives in terms of personal choice. Regardless of the favored option, all the competing views are still considered to be biblical.

In response, Roman Catholicism has argued since at least the rise of Protestantism in the sixteenth century that some of its beliefs come from the Bible, none of its beliefs contradict it, and other beliefs come from sources outside the Bible (namely oral tradition). Orthodox Christians will often adopt this Roman Catholic approach when conversing with Protestants, despite the many disagreements between Orthodoxy and Roman Catholicism on the subject of Church authority.

The purpose of this book is to provide at least a basic understanding of what the Bible is, where it came from, and how to read it as an Orthodox Christian. After all, the way to overcome all these issues is to truly know the Bible. And the way to know the Bible is to learn how to read and understand it.

Beyond its usefulness in biblical discussions and the spiritual benefits of reading the Bible, however, is something just as important: The Bible offers spiritual sustenance. Being able to read and understand it is a source of joy and strength that Christians should seek out.

Except where noted, all translations of the Scriptures and other ancient sources are my own. That said, no translation is ever perfect, and that includes the ones I present. As this book discusses, translation is more an art than a science, especially when working with ancient languages that are constructed very differently from the English language. Sometimes, in making a particular point or argument, a translation may need to be very precise about a certain word or explain that the same word is used in two places. For a variety of reasons, however, a standard English translation may lack that precision. For all these reasons it seems best to translate afresh for significant quotations.

CHAPTER ONE

What Is the Bible?

T HE WORD "BIBLE" IS A transliteration of the Greek word *biblia*, which means "books." It refers to a book as a literary unit rather than to its format, which might be a scroll, a codex, or what we think of as a modern book. "Holy Bible," therefore, essentially means "holy books."

The collection of all these texts into one modern book is a relatively recent historical development, as we will discuss in a subsequent chapter. The more proper term to describe these texts is "the Scriptures." The word "Scriptures" is a transliteration from the Latin meaning "the things that are written." This Latin term was drawn from the usual way in which the New Testament quotes authoritative texts: they are generally preceded by the words "It is written."

As people in the modern age, we tend to underestimate the value of the written word. We live not only after the advent of the printing press but in an age of self-publishing and ebooks. When the biblical texts were written, however, literacy rates were extremely low, and putting something into writing was a costly and difficult proposition. A class of professional scribes composed and copied texts, but their services and the basic materials necessary to produce a manuscript were quite expensive. According to some estimates, a single copy of a text roughly the length of the Book of Romans in the New Testament would have cost the equivalent of five thousand dollars. Beyond the expense, certain texts were preserved at the temple in Jerusalem, giving them an even higher status and authority.

A written text in the ancient world was seen as a literary monument. A significant difference existed between the phrases "It is said" and "It is written." The Scriptures, then, at the most basic level, are those things that have been written down and preserved from former times. But we do not consider everything that was written down in former or even ancient times to be Scripture in this sense. In our present day, archaeological discoveries have given us texts from Sumer, Egypt, Babylon, and other places that are as old as or older than the texts that are part of the Bible. The particular "written things" that make up the Bible are distinguished and set apart from all others.

Inspiration

"FOR NEVER WAS A PROPHECY brought by the will of man, but men, being carried by the Holy Spirit, spoke from God" (2 Pet. 1:21). In this sentence, St. Peter describes the way in which the Scriptures came to be as well as what distinguishes them from all other literary compositions. The latter come from the minds, wills, and intentions of human beings. The Scriptures, on the other hand, find their ultimate origin in the will and intentions of God Himself.

Later in his letter, St. Peter adds the letters of St. Paul to the existing body of Scripture (2 Pet. 3:16). Saint Paul, writing to St. Timothy, states that all Scripture has been breathed out by God (2 Tim. 3:16). Christ Himself, citing the Scriptures, asks the Sadducees, "Have you not read what was said to you by God?" (Matt. 22:31).

This does not mean that the human authors of the various books of the Bible were uninvolved in their composition. People sometimes imagine that the authors fell into a trance and woke up to find a finished work in front of them. Or that they heard a voice in their minds and dutifully wrote down each word as it was uttered. This is simply not the case. In the New Testament, varying levels of Greek fluency between the authors are apparent. In addition, different authors write in different styles, use different vocabulary, and use more or less complex grammatical constructions.

The Old Testament, particularly in the Hebrew, offers a more uniform style. Its cohesiveness is due to later editing and translation. But even that similarity of style doesn't erase the differences in vocabulary, which reveal that the books' various authors wrote at different points in time over the space of more than a thousand years.

In order to understand in what way the Scriptures are inspired, it is important to recognize also that each individual text was not the product of a single moment of composition. This is particularly clear in the case of the Old Testament. While the Pentateuch (the first five books of the Bible) is Mosaic in origin, the language and style in which our earliest manuscripts are written did not exist at the time of Moses. This means at the very least that these texts have been translated and edited.

The Book of Psalms likewise consists of independent poetic units. The oldest ones are attributed to Moses; others clearly date from the time after the exile in Babylon nearly a thousand years later. Within the Book of Psalms are five "books," which represent smaller collections of psalms that were later brought together to form the biblical book as we now know it. Even within that finished book, however, the numbering of the psalms differs in Hebrew and Greek because some psalm texts are united in one and divided in the other.

We are told that Isaiah's prophecies were written and collected by his disciples (Is. 8:16–20). Isaiah did not write the book as a single act, and there is good evidence in our present Book of Isaiah that it consists of more than one collection of his prophecies.

The Book of Jeremiah exists in the original Hebrew in two distinct forms, which are approximately one-third different in their texts. In addition we have the other Jeremiah material: the Book of Lamentations, the Book of Baruch, and Jeremiah's epistle.

That the Christian Old Testament is the product of a millennium-and-a-half-long process is therefore obvious to the honest observer of the material. That the New Testament is the product of a similar process is perhaps less obvious. In fact, as we will see, many modern arguments regarding the nature of the Scriptures are based on ignoring this fact about the New Testament and then arguing from that mistaken viewpoint concerning the whole of the Scriptures. Moderns tend to imagine St. Paul sitting down to write his letters to the churches, or St. John sitting down to write his Gospel, and composing it in a single afternoon. This is not accurate. We know that St. Paul did not handwrite the bulk of his epistles, because he states at certain points that he is writing "with his own hand" and that this can be seen by the size of the letters (Gal. 6:11; 2 Thess. 3:17).

Normally, St. Paul employed a sort of secretary known as an *amanuensis* (Rom. 16:22; 1 Cor. 16:21; Col. 4:18). The typical process for the composition of such an epistle would have been for St. Paul to deliver it orally to the secretary, who would write it down and provide corrections for style and grammar. The author would then review the text, making any corrections he deemed necessary, before another person delivered the letter. This person would read the letter aloud to the community to which it was written and be expected to answer questions regarding its content.

By the end of the first century, St. Paul's letters had been gathered into a collection and were circulating in that collected form. All our extant manuscripts of the epistles come from this collection. This collection also involved editing. What we now call 2 Corinthians, for example, includes at least two of St. Paul's epistles edited together. Although many of the Fathers believed that someone other than St. Paul wrote the Epistle to the Hebrews, it is still traditionally ascribed to St. Paul because it has circulated, from around AD 100, as part of this collection.

What we have said here about St. Paul's epistles could be said for the other New Testament texts as well. The four Gospels and the General Epistles also were circulated as collections from at least the year AD 150. Saint Luke says in the beginning of his Gospel that he compiled information from various eyewitness sources to compose it. Additionally, two versions of Luke and Acts, of considerably different lengths, are found among biblical manuscripts. One common thesis as to how this came about is that the longer form of these texts represents a sort of "second edition" also written by St. Luke.

Thus it is not enough to state that a theoretical "original" version of the texts that comprise the Scriptures was inspired or breathed out by the Holy Spirit. In the case of most of the texts in question, it is difficult even to determine what this "original" text would be. The text as it came to exist in the author's mind? What left his mouth? What was first written? What was produced following the initial edit? Later edits? The text as it existed in the earliest collections? The text as it existed at some particular point in the history of the Church? The text produced by a particular translation? Unless this hypothetical text is one that actually exists and can be agreed upon in its details, then any claims about it are essentially meaningless.

In order for the inspiration of Scripture to be meaningful, it requires that the Holy Spirit carry men along the entire process that produced the Scriptures. This includes speaking, writing, editing, copying, translating, and compiling. The inspiration of Scripture is the affirmation that, while humans performed all these tasks at various times and in various places, they were guided in so doing by the Spirit of God. This is what gives the Bible its unique character among all the other books and ancient texts that exist and that are the product of human activity. This is also the reason the handling of the Scriptures—their reading, studying, preaching, and meditation—is always accompanied by prayer.

Inerrancy

BEGINNING IN THE EIGHTEENTH CENTURY in Protestant Europe, the application of scientific rationalism to the study of the biblical text began to cast doubt on the reality of what were described as "supernatural" or "miraculous" events in the Scriptures. A renewed attention to the idea of laws by which the universe customarily functions, discernible through human reason and the scientific method, had created a category of claimed events that did not obey these laws.

These were first designated as miracles, acts of God within time that deviated from natural law. Through the lens of scientific rationalism, however, these same events became a springboard for some rather bizarre explanations. Christ walking on the water was explained as Him traversing a hidden sandbar. The feeding of the five thousand was accomplished by people choosing to follow Christ's example and share the food they previously had kept hidden. Christ raising a person from the dead was attributed to His superior wisdom, knowing that the person had swooned or was in a coma and not actually dead. It didn't take long, of course, for interpreters to reject these explanations and simply categorize the stories as pious fictions. Thomas Jefferson famously produced a much-shortened New Testament by removing all such events as unbelievable to a modern person.[1]

This new "scientific" approach to Scripture continued to be used throughout the nineteenth century, again particularly in Protestant Europe, in the dissection of the Christian Scriptures. Especially in the German universities, the Old Testament was pulled apart, the individual books broken up, sometimes verse by verse, and attributed to discrete sources from a variety of time periods, all of them centuries after the events they

---

1   A copy of the "Jefferson Bible" is given to every incoming member of the United States Congress.

describe. In this way, the Scriptures were seen as ahistorical and the sources from which they are derived as being in conflict with one another.

The New Testament documents, likewise, were asserted to be entirely pseudonymous and mostly the product of the second century rather than the first. This, it was argued, gave time for hypothetical exaggerations. Rather than studying the texts, early archaeology (primarily in the British holdings in the Middle East) focused on pursuing the "real" history that might lie somewhere behind the text. In the Old Testament, this took the form of rewriting the history of the ancient nation of Israel. In the New Testament, it became a quest for the "historical Jesus," who scholars believed was someone quite different from the "Christ of faith."

Having dominated European universities for the better part of a century, this mode of scholarship arrived at American universities in the early twentieth century and became the prevailing method of biblical study at universities such as Harvard and Princeton. This development generated a strong counterreaction from religiously conservative American Protestants. The resistance coalesced in the publication of a series of tracts entitled "The Fundamentals." These tracts defended the truth of various aspects of Christian doctrine, from Christ's miracles and His Virgin Birth to the reality of the Exodus from Egypt and the historical existence of Adam, Eve, and King David. Those who adhered to these doctrines became known as "fundamentalists" and later as "evangelical fundamentalists." The former title related to their desire to defend what they saw as the Christian gospel.

In the midst of this controversy the word "inerrancy" was coined as an overarching term to describe the differences between the two groups under one head. The conservative Protestants argued that the Scriptures are inerrant, or without error, in all that they teach and proclaim. Liberal Protestants, on the other hand, viewed the Scriptures as important documents but believed that, as ancient texts, they embodied all the foibles of human beings from the eras in which they were written, and so they needed to be corrected or improved on in places. These respective views became increasingly polarized throughout the twentieth century.

Both "fundamentalist" and "liberal" became pejorative labels, with each side questioning whether the other could rightly be called Christian. The side embracing inerrancy, because they found themselves consistently defending the literal historicity of the Old Testament, became predominantly focused on arguing for six literal, twenty-four-hour days of creation, a young Earth, a global flood, the dating of the Exodus, and similar elements of the Old Testament narratives. The more theologically liberal side came to be dominated by social and political concerns, its proponents seeking to focus on the reconstructed philosophy of the historical Jesus. This, in turn, served to push the theologically conservative side of the debate toward opposite political positions and movements, deeply embedding in American party politics a debate that began as a discussion of biblical interpretation.

The Orthodox Church, for the most part, was not a party to these debates, though occasionally it was an onlooker. It has always been the teaching of the Orthodox Church that the Scriptures do not contain errors. However, the Church never treated as an end in itself the demonstration that various texts of the Old Testament have some foundation in archaeology or that certain passages in the Gospels that seem to contradict one another can be reconciled. In large part, this is because the Church has never approached the world on the basis of the Scriptures; rather, the Scriptures function internally, within the Church and her worship. To be a Christian within the Orthodox Church has never depended on believing in the historical veracity of certain portions of the Scriptures. Christianity is seen as a cohesive way of life that encompasses the whole of a person. Reading and meditating on the Scriptures forms an important part of that way of life, but it doesn't require defending the proposition that the Scriptures are without error. Of the two sides, the teaching of the Orthodox Church regarding the Scriptures is more closely allied with the concept of inerrancy; however, the Orthodox Church has a fundamentally different view of the place the Scriptures hold in the life of the Church.

Sola Scriptura

ONE OF THE FOUNDING DOCTRINES of Protestantism, proceeding from the Reformation of the sixteenth century, is *sola scriptura*. This literally means "Scripture alone." As traditionally elaborated by Protestants, this is the idea that the Scriptures are the sole, infallible rule for the faith and life of Christians. This statement, however, was formulated to refute doctrine taught by the Roman Catholicism at the time of the Protestant Reformation, and so it can be properly understood only against this background. As with the inerrancy issue, this debate is fundamentally one between two groups outside the Orthodox Church. While there are points of congruence between the teaching of the Orthodox Church and the positions of one or the other side, the teaching of the Church as a whole supersedes the terms of the debate and is identical to neither side.

In terms of the classical formulation of sola scriptura, Western Christians are in agreement that there are three basic sources of authority in the life of the Church. The dispute between Roman Catholics and Protestants relates to which of these authorities is preeminent. These three sources of authority are the Scriptures, tradition, and the teaching authority of the Church. Sola scriptura is the view that, of these three separate sources of authority, Scripture is preeminent. The teachings of any church authority, whether it be an ordained individual, a council, or a statement of faith, must be tested against Scripture. Traditions that come to exist in various churches must likewise be tested against Scripture on an ongoing basis to determine their validity. Both tradition and church authority are capable of being, and often are, wrong.

Rome places the teaching authority of the Church, the magisterium, in the preeminent place. It is the teaching authority that defines what is and isn't Scripture and how it is to be interpreted. The teaching authority also defines what is and isn't a valid part of the received tradition and how that tradition is to be interpreted and applied.

What both of these Western views have in common is that they view the revelation of God as primarily discursive, as a series of truths or propositions that are communicated to human beings. The theological task in the West has historically been to arrange these true propositions into logical arguments and to use them to construct further theological doctrines. These later constructions may be called "good and necessary inferences from Scripture" by Protestants or "the progress of doctrine" by Rome, but the fundamental project is the same.

Orthodox Christianity from the New Testament on, however, has seen the revelation of God to be contained in the Person of Jesus Christ. Christ is the Truth. Therefore, the only way to come to know God is to come to know Christ. There is an important distinction here between knowing God and knowing *about* God. While the West speaks of coming to know certain things about God from natural revelation in Creation, certain other things through the Scriptures, certain other things through oral tradition, and so on, the East has instead emphasized coming to know God experientially, by coming as a human person to know and be united with the Person of Christ.

The question then becomes, how do we come to know Christ in the Church? As Christ expressed it in the Gospel of John, "When the Comforter comes, whom I myself will send to you from the Father, the Spirit of Truth who proceeds from the Father, that one will bear witness concerning me. And you also will bear witness, because you have been with me from the beginning" (15:26–27). Here Christ describes two witnesses who will testify to His Person, through whom He will be known in the future after He has ascended to the right hand of the Father. The first is the Holy Spirit. The life of the Holy Spirit in the Church, from His descent at Pentecost to the present day, is what is called Holy Tradition in the Orthodox Christian Faith. Saint John's theme throughout this passage has been that Christ's followers will come to know Him through the working of the Holy Spirit. This life of the Spirit is accurately referred to as "tradition" because it is perfectly unified throughout the Church and throughout the Church's history: it is the same Spirit bringing human persons to know the same Christ.

The second witness this passage refers to is the testimony of the apostles themselves—those who were with Christ from the beginning and knew Him directly and intimately. The earliest Fathers gave the title "the memoirs of the Apostles" to the texts that would become known as the New Testament. Luke introduces his Gospel by writing, "just as it was handed down [literally, "traditioned"] to us by those who from the beginning were eyewitnesses and servants of the Word" (1:2). The second witness is, therefore, the Scriptures themselves.

By here citing two witnesses, Christ is appealing to a principle laid out originally in the Torah: that any truth in court must be established by the testimony of two witnesses (see Deut. 19:15). For these two witnesses' testimony to be valid, that testimony must be identical. If they tell different stories, it is rejected. Therefore, it is necessary to recognize that the testimony of the Holy Spirit within the Church and the testimony of the Scriptures is at all times identical. We should expect this if both of these are bringing us to know the same Person: the living Jesus Christ. The two cannot be separated from one another and therefore cannot be pitted against each other, nor one placed above the other.

Rather than saying that the Orthodox Church "rejects" the position of sola scriptura, it is more correct to say that the Orthodox Church does not hold to the definition of God's revelation—of separate, competing authorities in the Church—that makes sola scriptura possible. The Scriptures are not a manual on how to live a moral life or how to organize the Church as an institution. The Scriptures are the means by which we come to know the Risen Christ, always through the working of the Holy Spirit.

CHAPTER TWO

What Is in the Bible?

T HE BIBLE IS NOT A single, uniform document, but a collection of texts composed, edited, copied, translated, and circulated over the course of more than thirteen centuries. In the previous chapter, we described the way the texts that make up the Christian Scriptures differ from other ancient texts in the context of inspiration. The Holy Spirit was responsible for bringing these writings into existence through human authors and editors. Once they existed, however, and as they were shaped over time, they had to be gathered together as the Scriptures in order to eventually become the Bible we have today.

Most importantly, out of all the texts in circulation in the Jewish and Christian communities, only certain texts were ultimately included in the canon of Scripture. A literary canon is a set of texts that exercise an authoritative role in a community. This definition applies both to extrabiblical uses of the term and to the Bible itself. Determining which texts are canonical is an objective process. A text is either authoritative for a given community or it is not. With regard to the Christian Church, human preferences and principles do not guide this curation. Rather, the books that have come to hold canonical authority within the Church are those that bear the inspiration of the Holy Spirit.

The issue of canon is often taken for granted in our modern world. At the beginning of our Bibles, we find a table of contents listing the books contained therein. These are the "books of the Bible" as far as we are concerned. The problem with this simple answer is that reality complicates it. We may become aware that the list of books in our Orthodox Bible is not the same as the list in Roman Catholic Bibles or Protestant Bibles. We may watch a documentary that refers to texts which were "banned from the Bible," with the implication that someone, somewhere, attempted to suppress or hide the contents of those texts. Frequently, some new text from the ancient world with some connection to biblical books or figures will be rediscovered, and news stories will claim that these discoveries will somehow change Christianity forever.

We have become accustomed to thinking of the Bible as a single book between two covers. For the average Christian to own a Bible (or several) and to be able to read it regularly and privately is a recent historical development. Prior to the invention of the printing press, Bibles existed as various codices. A codex was a sort of book in which many leaves of parchment or vellum (cleaned and prepared animal skins) were tied together between two covers. The codex as a form of written text originally became popular in the Christian communities of the early centuries. Prior to this, most biblical texts circulated in the form of papyrus leaves or rolled scrolls.

Only in rare cases do early Christian codices resemble our modern Bibles. Those extant for our study are evenly split between continuous texts, which is the form of the books as they are published in our Bibles, and lectionaries, which divide the texts into a series of daily readings. The Gospel and Epistle books used in Orthodox churches take the latter form. It is extremely rare to find a codex of either type containing the entirety of the Old and New Testaments. Individual codices will contain the Gospels, the Epistles, the Psalter, or various portions of the Old Testament. There is no suggestion that any of these individual codices comprise the entirety of the texts that hold authority in the church in which that codex was discovered.

Further, because of the cost of copying and binding codices, other texts are often included in any given historical codex. Additions include hymns, prayers, and even entire devotional texts. It is sometimes wrongly assumed that if something is found within a particular codex, the community in which it was found must have considered it to be a part of the canonical Scriptures. As just one example, the early Greek codex of the Old Testament that is used as the base text for most printed Greek Old Testaments includes the nine biblical odes as sung at Matins services in the Church. The ninth of these odes is the Magnificat, the hymn of the Theotokos from the first chapter of St. Luke's Gospel. Certainly, no one believed that St. Luke's Gospel, or this single chapter, was part of the Old Testament. This assumption would be like a Christian living centuries from now finding one of our modern study Bibles and concluding that twenty-first-century Christians believed a certain set of maps and a series of introductions and notes to be canonical.

There was also never a point in time when a group of people sat down and decided which texts would and would not be included in a book called "the Bible." Unfortunately, a number of misconceptions exist surrounding how the canon of the

Christian Scriptures was formed. The most common of these is that the Old Testament already existed as a unit, the Hebrew Bible, before the advent of Christ. The story continues that Christians then took over this single literary unit and added on to it to create the New Testament. The most common misconception concerning the New Testament is that the canon of twenty-seven books was decided upon, by some sort of vote, at the Council of Nicea in AD 325. Both of these are simply untrue.

The Old Testament Canon

BECAUSE IT PRECEDES THE NEW Testament in our modern Bibles and dates from an earlier period of history, it is sometimes assumed that the Christian Old Testament, or the Hebrew Bible, existed as an agreed-upon unit before the New Testament was composed. This is not the case. First, the codex format was not used for the texts of the Old Testament in the first century AD. These texts were still copied and kept on individual scrolls. A synagogue would have a Torah scroll. A well-endowed synagogue would have other books, most likely the Psalms and Isaiah. Only in major cities such as Jerusalem or Alexandria did Jewish communities have access to the full range of the Scriptures in written form.

Therefore, certain texts exercised canonical authority in Jewish communities, but no authoritative collections or even lists of these texts were available to the average person. Worshippers knew these words were authoritative because they were read aloud at the synagogue. While certain texts were uncontroversial in their authority with Jewish believers, others were debated or even unknown to the vast majority of pious Jewish people. The idea of a canon existed, but trained rabbinical teachers of the first century would not have agreed on its exact boundaries. They would also have been hard pressed to offer objective, incontrovertible proof that their particular opinion on the issue was correct.

Modern scholars sometimes point to the collection of scrolls that was kept at the temple in Jerusalem as the basis for the idea of a first-century Old Testament canon, but this is problematic for several reasons. While some texts were kept in the temple and others were not, the list of those that were does not perfectly conform to the canon of the Hebrew Bible or of any major Christian body's Old Testament. A number of books that would later be a part of all these canons, such as Ecclesiastes and Esther, were still the subject of debate even at the Jerusalem temple in the first century.

Additionally, while the temple in Jerusalem was the spiritual center of Jewish ritual and religious life throughout the world, the situation in the first century made this list inaccessible and irrelevant to the greater number of Jewish communities at the time. Many Jews lived in diaspora all across the Mediterranean. Those who had the financial means would go to great effort to travel to Jerusalem for the major feasts as often as possible, but these wealthy people were the minority of the world's Jewish believers. Even those who did travel to Jerusalem were not given access to the scrolls kept in the temple. And those who might have been able to gain access were not literate in the biblical Hebrew and Aramaic in which those scrolls were written. Only those with advanced scribal training of a type that could only be obtained in and around Jerusalem would have been able to identify and read these scrolls. At this time, it was far more common to hear the Scriptures read in Greek translation at synagogues outside of Judea proper, even as nearby as Galilee.

Additionally, a large number of Jewish communities in the first century outright rejected the authority of the temple, for various reasons. Many Jewish groups objected to the fact that the building of the temple complex had been initiated by Herod, a non-Jew and a person of questionable morality, and continued by equally immoral but less talented sons. Others objected that the high-priestly family that controlled the temple was from the party of the Sadducees and did not descend from the Levitical family of Zadok, who were to serve as priests of the new temple according to prophecy. Others believed that because the glory of God had not visibly returned to the temple, God had rejected it. Others pointed to the fact that the ark of the covenant was not there. These signs and the fact that Judea was still under foreign oppression by the Romans meant that the exile had not ended and the temple was therefore illicit.

Whatever the reason for the rejection, the outcome was the same: If the communities could not trust the temple's leadership, they could not accept their authority to decide which texts were canonical. Many Jewish communities outside Jerusalem assembled their own collections of authoritative texts, such as the Dead Sea Scrolls at Qumran.

The Torah

THE FOUNDATION OF THE OLD TESTAMENT canon, and of the concept of a biblical canon, is the Torah, or the Pentateuch. Though composed of five books, the Torah has been considered a unit since the earliest stages of Israelite history that are accessible to us. Genesis, Exodus, Leviticus, Numbers, and Deuteronomy represent a charter for the national and religious identity of the people of Israel. In later books of the Old Testament, as well as the New Testament and other related literature, these books are often identified with the figure of Moses, and traditionally, they have their origin with the person of Moses himself. This association has sometimes been pressed further, to the idea that Moses authored these five books, as we now have them, in their entirety. There are numerous difficulties with this, chief among them the fact that the earliest extant forms of these texts were written in a language that did not exist in Moses' day. It is more correct then to speak of a Mosaic origin, knowing that Moses did indeed engage in scribal activity, and that through centuries of compilation and translation, the Torah emerged.

The Pentateuch as it currently stands shows evidence of various stages of later editing. For example, Genesis 14:4 states that Abram pursued the kings who had taken his nephew, Lot, captive "as far as Dan." Not only was this city not known as Dan in Abram's time, but it was not called that centuries later in Moses' time either. The city was renamed Dan after it was illicitly taken by the tribe of Dan following the Israelite conquest of Canaan (Josh. 19:47). Clearly, a later editor or copyist updated the name of the city in Genesis so that readers would understand the geography. In other places, the editing is even more transparent: both an earlier and a later name for a place are given.

The most famous theory regarding the composition and editing of the Pentateuch is the "documentary hypothesis," which sought to discover the sources that Moses used to compile the text. This theory was originally constructed to defend the idea that Moses was sole author of the Pentateuch. In its later development by critical scholars, the theory has become the primary means for removing the composition of the Torah from Moses' era, a decision often accompanied by a denial of his existence, let alone literary activity.

In its classic form, the documentary hypothesis posits four sources, labeled J, E, D, and P. These are abbreviations for the Yahwist, Elohist, Deuteronomist, and Priestly sources. The first two are said to be distinguished by the preference of referring to God by the name "Yahweh" or the name "Elohim" in Hebrew. The third is the author of the Book of Deuteronomy as a separate composition. The priestly source is generally considered to be a later redactor, or editor, who was part of the priestly caste in ancient Israel and made edits and additions generally assumed to support the authority of the priesthood within Israel.

As tends to happen with such theories, variations of this breakdown of sources became nearly endlessly complex over succeeding generations. Scholars labeled multiple speculative sources in each of the four categories. The different sources became layers of editorial activity piled up like sediment. Portions of biblical verses, sometimes consisting of only two or three words, were assigned to different layers of activity in different centuries. Though journal articles must still be published and dissertations must still be written, discussions regarding the documentary hypothesis have become considerably more restrained. The complexity of the ways in which God is discussed in the Torah has made the delineation of the J and E sources dubious. The Book of Deuteronomy is a self-contained, structured work that does not correspond to the other four books of the Pentateuch. Certainly, based on its high level of literacy, we may conclude that many of the hands that worked on the text of the Torah throughout its various stages were priestly.

It is also incontrovertible that the Pentateuch interacts with other sources. Particularly in the first eleven chapters of Genesis but continuing throughout, the text comments on, reinterprets, and sometimes even inverts the traditions of Egypt, Canaan, and Mesopotamia. All of this is useful information that can assist in understanding the text of the Torah. Strictly speaking, however, it is not relevant to the way in which the Pentateuch functions in the Christian Church. It is the completed text, as it was received into the Church by the apostles, that holds authority within Christian communities, not any hypothetical sources or earlier stages of the text.

Within the Orthodox Church, this has always been understood. Greek-speaking synagogues followed by Greek-speaking churches have received and used a particular third-century BC translation of the Pentateuch, the Septuagint, authoritatively. This, despite the fact that no one proposes that Moses ever wrote anything in Greek. The identities of the authors and editors of a given text of Scripture are largely irrelevant to the Scripture's canonical authority. This is particularly clear in the Old Testament, where many portions were written and edited by completely unknown people.

The Pentateuch itself, as it now exists, describes the role that the Torah would come to play in the nation of Israel. The Book of Deuteronomy commands that the Torah be read publicly every seven years in the hearing of the people (Deut. 31:11). This is not just for the elders of Israel or other leading men. Rather, all the men, women, and children of Israel are to gather to hear it, as well as aliens and foreigners who may be present in Israel at the time, with the goal that they learn to fear God and to do the works required by the Torah (v. 12). The text is entrusted to the Levites, parallel to New Testament deacons, and the elders of the people (in Greek, *presbyters*), that they may read and teach it to all the people (v. 9). This pattern for the role of the Scriptures in the worship of the Church has endured throughout Christian history.

The Prophets

THE SECOND MAJOR COLLECTION OF texts that make up part of the Christian Old Testament is the prophetic corpus, sometimes referred to simply as "the Prophets." Within this group of texts, however, there is a further distinction between the "Former Prophets" and the "Latter Prophets" or, in more modern categorizations based on genre, the "historical books" and the "prophetic books." The earlier set of texts, consisting generally of Joshua, Judges, Ruth, 1 and 2 Samuel, 1 and 2 Kings (or, in the Greek naming, 1—4 Kingdoms), and 1 and 2 Chronicles, are books of third-person history, describing the history of the nation of Israel from its entrance into the land of Canaan following Moses' death to the Babylonian conquest of the Southern Kingdom of Judah and their exile circa 586 BC.

Describing these texts as historical, however, does not mean that they are written in the way we write history today. The chief difference is that in our contemporary world there is at least a pretense to objectivity when history is written. The stated intent is to simply communicate facts about what took place without choosing sides in all but the worst atrocities of history, which of course must be condemned. The Former Prophets, on the other hand, describe the history of Israel with undisguised bias, reading that history from the perspective of the Torah, both praising those in Israel's history who were obedient and harshly criticizing the disobedient.

As just one example, Omri was, based on our archaeological discoveries, one of the most important kings in the history of Israel. He established a powerful dynasty, made alliances with the Phoenicians that brought great wealth and prosperity to the Kingdom of Israel, and laid the basis for a new capital city. The other nations of the ancient Near East referred to Israel as "the House of Omri" for more than a century. In contrast, 1 Kings/3 Kingdoms contains eight verses dedicated to him. And these tell us that he was evil, worse than all before him, and committed abominations (16:25–26). We are then told that if we want to read about all the things he said and did, these can be found in his official annals (v. 27). They are of no concern to the biblical author, as Omri was such a wicked king.

This bias in telling the history of Israel in these books is grounded deeply in the perspective of the Torah in general, and Deuteronomy in particular. For this reason, scholars have long referred to the series of texts from Joshua to 2 Kings/4 Kingdoms as "Deuteronomistic History." Deuteronomy, in its concluding chapters, lays out blessings that will come to Israel for obedience and curses that will befall her for disobedience. In the subsequent historical books, we see how these promises and warnings played out over time.

This collection of texts also reveals the first, though by no means the only, example of texts that describe the same set of narratives differently. There is a great overlap between 1 and

2 Kings/3 and 4 Kingdoms and 1 and 2 Chronicles. In general, many of these differences occur because of the two authors' variations in themes. As just discussed, the author of Kings/ Kingdoms describes the history of Israel from the perspective of Deuteronomy's prophecies regarding her future. First and Second Chronicles, on the other hand, describe the history of Israel and Judah from the perspective of the Davidic monarchy of Judah, which the Chronicler is confident will produce the Messiah. Both of these are valid perspectives on the realities of Israel's history.

Jews and Christians of the pre-Christian and early Christian centuries considered the Latter Prophets, or prophetic books proper—though very different in genre and style from the Former Prophets or historical books—to be of a piece. They understood this entire body of literature to describe that period of Israel's history after the death of Moses, the first and paradigmatic prophet for the Israelites, during which God sent prophets to His people to call them back to the teachings of the Torah. The New Testament will often describe all of Israel's history as a nation as "the time of the prophets," generally also commenting on the abuse and even martyrdom that these prophets endured. It was common in the first century to refer to the existing Scriptures as "the Law (Torah) and the Prophets."

The prophets proper, often called the literary (or writing) prophets, are better referred to as the "classical prophets." The prophets who appear in the Deuteronomistic history, such as Samuel, Nathan, Elijah, and Elisha are referred to as the "pre-classical prophets." The classical prophets are texts that account for those that bear the names of major prophets: Isaiah, Jeremiah, and Ezekiel. They also include what is sometimes called the "minor prophets." The following twelve texts are more properly referred to as the Twelve: Hosea, Joel, Amos, Obadiah, Jonah, Micah, Nahum, Habakkuk, Zephaniah, Haggai, Zechariah, and Malachi. These twelve shorter texts circulated in the ancient world on a single scroll referred to as the Book of the Twelve.

These texts vary in literary genre. All of them contain the prophetic utterances of the titular prophets recorded in written form. Some, however, such as Isaiah, Jeremiah, Ezekiel, and Jonah, contain substantial amounts of historical narrative as well. Jonah contains considerably more narrative than words of the prophet. Other texts in this group contain no narrative whatsoever, but only the prophet's recorded words. None of these documents claims to have been composed as a written work by the prophet whose name it bears. In fact, several of them identify another writer, such as Jeremiah's scribe Baruch, or the fact that Isaiah's disciples are said to have collected his prophecies after his death to form the Book of Isaiah (Is. 8:16). In the case of most of these books, the precise author remains, and likely will remain, unknown.

As mentioned, these two bodies of text, the Torah and the Prophets, formed the first two major divisions of the Hebrew Scriptures, and by the first century AD the broader Jewish world received them as authoritative. A handful of Jewish groups at the time, such as the Sadducees, accepted only the Torah, but even these broadly accepted the historical reliability of the Former Prophets and in broad strokes the eschatology of the Latter Prophets regarding the coming of a Messiah. The Torah represented God's teaching to His people revealed through the prophet Moses. The Prophets represented the authoritative history of God's dealing with Israel after the fulfillment of the Torah's promises, ending in Israel's exile.

The Writings

THE THIRD DIVISION OF THE Hebrew Scriptures, the Writings, is essentially a catchall. The Hebrew word *Ketuvim* means simply "things written" and is the equivalent of the word "Scriptures." The texts included in this category are widely divergent and include poetry and prose, sayings, collections, historical narrative, apocalypticism, and love song. These are essentially the "other" texts that came to hold importance and authority within the context of the life of Jewish communities. For these reasons, it is difficult to make any generalizations about this literature or even treat it as a "collection" per se.

Certain elements of the Writings were uncontroversial. The Psalms, for example, were treated not only as authoritative with regard to their use in worship, but also as doctrinally informative, as evidenced by the fact that the Book of Psalms is quoted more than any other in the New Testament. That said, the exact assortment and numbering of the Psalms took slightly different approaches in different Psalm collections. The Book of Psalms is in fact made up of five identified, smaller collections. A more well-known variation, on the other hand, is the difference in the numbering of most of the Psalms between the Hebrew and Greek collections. Despite variations in the arrangement of the collections, the content of the Psalms is, generally speaking, unvarying.

The status of the remainder of the texts that belong to the Writings as a subdivision is far less historically clear. Even in the first century AD disagreement continued about the authoritative status of certain books. Additionally, several of these texts existed in multiple forms, with different communities holding different versions to be authoritative. Christian communities resolved many of these disputes within the pre-existing Jewish communities by receiving certain books and certain versions of those books, yet some of these disputes regarding other books continued among Christians. This debate played out in the West with Protestant groups and Roman Catholic groups choosing opposing traditions that dated back to at least the third century in the West. In the Christian East, this issue has never been formally resolved, and there are a few texts that are considered authoritative in one local Orthodox church and not in another.

One major reason for these disagreements is that many of the texts included in this third canonical division of the Old Testament were written considerably later, after the exile in Babylon had concluded, beginning in the fifth century BC. From this period until the first century AD, hundreds of texts were written within Jewish communities. Judah's exile and return at the hands of the Babylonian and Persian empires had produced three great centers of Judaism: Judea, Egypt, and Mesopotamia. Beyond these major centers, smaller Jewish communities were scattered throughout the Persian Empire and the later Greek and Roman worlds. In addition to individual communities located in particular places, Jewish sects and schools of thought, such as the Pharisees, the Sadducees, the Essenes, and the Therapeutae, existed throughout these communities.

Within each community, certain texts held authority and constituted a canon. The discovery of the Dead Sea Scrolls has given us an example of one such community, located at Wadi

Qumran. Texts found at Qumran include the Torah and the Prophets, as well as a number of others that constitute their collection of Writings. Within this last category are texts that appear in the Hebrew Bible and Christian Old Testament, texts that are included in the latter but not the former, and texts such as 1 Enoch, which are included in neither. It also includes a set of texts peculiar to Qumran itself that deal with the founder of the community, their rule of life, and their particular interpretations of its scriptural texts. These texts evolved naturally within the community, and the same was true in other early Jewish and Christian communities.

The texts that make up the Writings in the Hebrew Bible and variations of the Christian Old Testament can be grouped into several categories. The first of these includes historical texts, roughly parallel in genre to those included in the Former Prophets. Some of these, such as Ezra, Nehemiah, and 1 and 2 Maccabees, provided historical narrative similar to the books of Kings/Kingdoms and Chronicles. Others, such as Esther, Tobit, and Judith, tell the stories of individual people more parallel to the Book of Ruth. Within this category, Esther represents a special case, in that it existed in the first century AD in at least two different versions. One of these versions ultimately became a part of the Hebrew Bible, and another became part of the Christian Old Testament.

Another category of literature within the Writings is wisdom literature. Possibly its best-known component is the Book of Proverbs. Proverbs is not a single book but a collection of wise sayings by different wise men, many of them identified within the text. A number of the collections in Proverbs are ascribed to Solomon, the king of Israel, and his name became associated with other wisdom texts as well, even if they did not bear his name. Ecclesiastes, the Song of Songs, and sometimes the Book of Wisdom are ascribed to Solomon, for example. Other Old Testament wisdom literature includes the Wisdom of Ben Sirach/Ecclesiasticus and the Book of Job.

Finally, the Writings include prophetic literature. In addition to the different collections of Jeremiah's prophecies present in the first century AD, several other texts were related to Jeremiah. His Lamentations over the destruction of Jerusalem eventually found universal acceptance by Jewish communities. Two other texts, the Epistle of Jeremiah, a letter ascribed to him, and the Book of Baruch, named for Jeremiah's scribe, were eventually accepted by most Christian communities. A series of other texts ascribed to Baruch in the ancient world never gained widespread acceptance as authoritative Scripture.

The Book of Daniel is also part of the writings. Daniel has its own unique textual history. The primary text is written partially in Hebrew and partially in Aramaic, making the transition between languages at seemingly arbitrary points. There is also a Greek version that is considerably longer, including additional narrative stories of Daniel. Further complicating this issue are attempts to date the Book of Daniel. The Greek translation of the text appears to date from the second century BC, and many scholars date the overall composition to that same time period. Others date the Hebrew/Aramaic version as early as the fifth century BC. Eventually, Jewish communities universally accepted the Hebrew/Aramaic version of Daniel, while the longer version found widespread acceptance in Christian communities.

The Formation of the Old Testament Canon

THE OLD TESTAMENT CANON IS formed from these three divisions: the Law, the Prophets, and the Writings. In Hebrew, these are the Torah, the Nevi'im, and the Ketuvim, often abbreviated as *Tanakh*. Every major Rabbinic Jewish and Christian community received the texts that make up the Law and the Prophets. Rabbinic Judaism eventually came to receive twenty-two canonical books as that religion formed following the destruction of the temple and then Jerusalem. These twenty-two books correspond to the thirty-nine books found in most English Old Testaments of American Protestant publication. In the Hebrew text, the twelve minor prophets are combined in one book, as are 1 and 2 Samuel, 1 and 2 Kings, 1 and 2 Chronicles, Judges/Ruth, and Ezra/Nehemiah. When the Fathers refer to twenty-two books, these are the books. All of them were also accepted by Christian communities, though, as noted, sometimes in different versions.

Western proponents, including most Protestant groups, typically cite one primary source in favor of accepting only these books received by Rabbinic Judaism as authoritative. This source is Flavius Josephus, the Jewish historian of the first century AD. In *Against Apion*, Josephus lists the books that he considers to constitute the Hebrew Scriptures. The Protestant argument then seeks to make Josephus's opinion a statement of what was universally held by all Jewish groups in the first century AD and therefore would have been received by all early Christians. To be fair, Josephus himself sought to universalize his opinion in the same way, writing:

Therefore, it naturally, even necessarily, follows . . . that we do not possess a myriad of divergent books which conflict with each other. Our books, those which are rightly recognized, are only twenty-two, and contain the record of all time. Of these, five are the books of Moses, made up of the laws and the traditional history from the beginning of humanity to the death of the lawgiver. . . . From the death of Moses until Artaxerxes, who succeeded Xerxes as king of Persia, the prophets who followed Moses wrote the history of the events of their own times in thirteen books. The remaining four books contain hymns to God and rules for the conduct of human life. From Artaxerxes to our own day the complete history has been written but has not been deemed worthy of equal credit with the earlier records, because of the failure of the succession of the prophets. . . . Although long ages have now passed, no one has dared either to add, to remove, or to alter a syllable. It is instinctual for every Judean, from the day of his birth, to recognize them as the proclamation of God, to obey them, and if need be willingly to die for them. (*Contra Apion*, 1.37–44)

Josephus does not merely express this grouping of texts to be the Scriptures according to his opinion or to be the canon as he received it from within his own community. Rather, he makes the claim that every single Jewish individual on earth, from birth, recognizes these and only these books. He further states that every one of those individuals obeys these Scriptures and is willing to die rather than violate a single command.

On its face, Josephus uses rather extreme hyperbole. Newborn infants have no opinion on the relative authority of various religious texts. Even a casual reading of the books that Josephus endorses reveals that the vast majority of Jewish people paid little attention to any of the commands of the Torah, let alone demonstrated a willingness to die for them. While Jewish martyrs existed, particularly in the Maccabean period as described in the books that Josephus here seems to marginalize, they were certainly never the majority any more than one can generalize from the Christian martyrs just how committed the majority of Christians were. Josephus also denies the editorial activity within the various texts that make up the Hebrew Bible, despite its being readily apparent even in translation.

Josephus was a member of the party of the Pharisees. His view on which Scriptures were authoritative within Jewish communities reflects this perspective, and the Pharisees would have agreed with him. But, even within Palestinian Judaism, not everyone was a Pharisee. Other religious parties existed in the first century within Palestine, and these parties had different collections of Scriptures that exercised authority within their communities. This is even more true of Jewish communities scattered across Egypt, Ethiopia, Mesopotamia, and the Roman world, reaching as far as Spain in that era. Josephus does not report objective fact but rather asserts that he and his fellows are right, over against competing parties. He goes a step further by asserting that everyone really knows that he is right, even if he or she won't admit it.

This proclamation by Josephus, then, while an important early witness to the understanding of one slice of Second Temple Judaism, is a flimsy basis on which to argue for the practice of the Christian Church in contemporary society. It is especially weak given that it conflicts with two millennia of Christian experience across the Christian world. Among early Christians, each community received a set of authoritative texts as its Old Testament, based on the texts that held authority in the preceding Jewish communities. Christian communities in Palestine received the canon of Palestinian Judaism; those in Egypt, Alexandrian Judaism; those in Ethiopia, Ethiopian Judaism.

Christian communities, therefore, often received more books of the Old Testament than these twenty-two (or thirty-nine in modern numbering) as authoritative. Which additional books they received and how they were received differed widely. Particularly in the East, Christians tended to recognize three categorizations of these texts: those that are read in the churches, those read in the home, and those not to be read. Some Christian communities received only these twenty-two as authoritative and to be read in the church, while they received others (and, in the case of the church in Ethiopia, a great many others) in a second category corresponding to those to be read in the home. Egypt also received an extensive list of books, but St. Athanasius, for example, consigned the Old Testament books of Tobit, Judith, Esther, Wisdom, and Ben Sirach, along with the Didache and Shepherd of Hermas, to such a second rank.[1] Saint Cyril of Jerusalem likewise wrote of the second rank of books that is neither to be read in the Church nor banned from reading, though he categorizes Old Testament books differently.[2] Saint Jerome did not consider any books beyond these twenty-two to be authoritative for the churches but translated a great many of them into Latin anyway as part of his Vulgate project.

---

1   *Paschal Letter,* 39.
2   *Catechetical Lectures,* 4, 33–36.

Certain Western churches set the limit strictly at the twenty-two accepted by Jewish communities.

This dispute would continue in the West up to and through the Protestant Reformation, during which Protestant and Roman Catholic churches defined the Old Testament canon on opposite sides. In the East, possibly because of its understanding of the third category of texts, no such active dispute exists, although variation in the exact borders of the Old Testament does continue to this day. The churches with the most expansive canons, the Ethiopian and Coptic churches (the former of which canons contains forty-six books), left communion with the Orthodox Church following the Council of Chalcedon in AD 451. This means that the variations in the East are a matter of only a few books. Further, the functional difference between "canonicity" and "deutero-canonicity" is negligible with respect to the Old Testament. Many books accepted as fully canonical within the Orthodox Church are never actually read publicly in liturgical contexts.

All Orthodox churches accept the twenty-two (or thirty-nine) universally accepted books: Genesis, Exodus, Leviticus, Numbers, Deuteronomy, Joshua, Judges, Ruth, 1 and 2 Samuel, 1 and 2 Kings/1—4 Kingdoms, 1 and 2 Chronicles, Ezra, Nehemiah, Esther, Job, Psalms, Proverbs, Ecclesiastes, Song of Songs, Isaiah, Jeremiah, Lamentations, Ezekiel, Daniel, Hosea, Joel, Amos, Obadiah, Jonah, Micah, Nahum, Habakkuk, Zephaniah, Haggai, Zechariah, and Malachi. Additionally, all Orthodox churches accept Tobit, Judith, 1 and 2 Maccabees, Wisdom, Ben-Sirach/Ecclesiasticus, Baruch, and the Epistle of Jeremiah. These books are also included in the Latin canon formalized by the Roman Catholic Church at the Council of Trent in the sixteenth century. Orthodox Churches also uniformly receive 1 Ezra (a text composed of portions of 1 Chronicles and Ezra), the Prayer of Manasseh, Psalm 151, and 3 Maccabees. Finally, the old Georgian text of the Old Testament includes 4 Ezra and 4 Maccabees, and through this text, these books became part of the Slavonic canon.[3]

As already mentioned, there are not, nor have there been, any active debates concerning these borders of the Old Testament canon in the East. This means that there has been no effort by local Orthodox churches to compel other local churches to receive texts into their Old Testament that they have not already received. Nor have there been efforts by local churches to compel other churches to reject books that they themselves have not received. Therefore, in the Orthodox Church, the precise list of the books in a Christian's Old Testament is a function of his or her community and the traditional biblical and liturgical language of that community.

The New Testament Canon

AS IS THE CASE WITH the Old Testament, the canon of the New Testament formed organically in the early Christian communities who received these texts from the apostles and their companions who wrote them. The primary obstacle to understanding the process by which we received our New Testament canon is not so much a lack of knowledge or misunderstanding as it is actual disinformation, conspiracy theory, and agendas

---

3   These books are often placed in an appendix, though the exact authoritative status of an appendix is not well defined beyond a general form of deutero-canonicity, or secondary canonicity.

regarding the characterization of the early Christian Church, her bishops, and her exercise of authority in the earliest period.

When asked when these twenty-seven books were canonized as the New Testament, many will answer that canonization happened at the Council of Nicea. Some will present this event as the bishops looking at a vast array of texts, including but not limited to the twenty-seven that would be accepted, and voting on which ones would and wouldn't be in "the Bible." Others will say that there wasn't a vote, but the bishops discussed the matter and arrived together at some set of criteria—usually including the apostolic origin of a text and a few others—by which they judged all these books and decided which were "in" and which were "out." From this kind of imagery, Roman Catholic apologists will assert that the authority of the books of the canon, therefore, rests on the authority of the bishops—particularly the bishop of Rome—who chose them. Often it is then said that Constantine, following the council, went on a sort of book-burning rampage, attempting to destroy all those other books besides the twenty-seven in order to conceal their contents.

The main problem with this approach is that it is grounded entirely in fiction. The canon of the New Testament was not discussed at Nicea in AD 325. Therefore, there was no vote, the bishops assembled no criteria, and certainly no subsequent book burning occurred. While this story has provided grist for novelists like Dan Brown and for the makers of cable television documentaries about "secret, lost books of the Bible," it cannot be taken seriously from a historical perspective.

Like the Old Testament, the New Testament is composed of a collection of independent texts. Unlike the Old Testament, all the texts of the New Testament were written over a relatively short period of time, roughly fifty years in the latter part of the first century AD. In the nineteenth and twentieth centuries, the dating of some of the texts of the New Testament was widely contested by scholars who held to an evolutionary view of Christian theology. In more recent times, textual finds and other considerations have produced a general agreement to this fact. For example, St. John's Gospel was, in the past, frequently pushed back as far as the middle of the second century in its composition. Today, a fragment of that Gospel is the oldest known New Testament manuscript and shows that this text must have been composed by the end of the first century.

Saint Paul is widely accepted by all scholars to have died by martyrdom in the mid-60s AD. There is therefore a consensus that he wrote his epistles between about AD 45 and that date. Some scholars dispute the Pauline authorship of several of these letters, but even they typically accept that the texts were written by St. Paul's immediate circles and the first generation of his followers, placing them in the latter part of the first century. There is likewise a consensus that the other epistles within the New Testament also were written in the late first century.

As already mentioned, St. John's Gospel, nearly universally considered by Church tradition and modern scholarship to be the latest Gospel, was written before the end of the first century. Saint Mark's Gospel is widely considered to have been the first written.[4] The early Fathers uniformly testify that St. Mark was a

---

4   A wide variety of theories attempt to explain how the Gospels of St. Matthew, St. Mark, and St. Luke relate to each other. Because St. Luke makes reference to using several written sources, he is widely considered to have written last. Saint Matthew's Gospel, as we now possess it, shows signs of clear literary

disciple of St. Peter at Rome and wrote his Gospel based on St. Peter's preaching and remembrances of Christ. Saint Irenaeus of Lyons, in the second century, gives the additional information that St. Mark did this after the deaths of Ss. Peter and Paul in the mid-60s. Based on this early testimony, scholars have traditionally dated St. Mark's Gospel to about AD 69.[5] Saint Irenaeus likewise gives us the most precise date for any of the New Testament texts when he tells us that St. John received the vision that became the Book of Revelation near the end of the reign of the emperor Domitian, AD 95.[6]

How, then, did the New Testament texts come together, and when? We know, from the writings of St. Irenaeus and others, and from actual textual discoveries, that the four Gospels, Matthew, Mark, Luke, and John, were being bound together in codices and used exclusively in churches by the middle part of the second century, that is, the AD 150s. Saint Irenaeus points out that this is the case in cities like Rome and Antioch, not because at that early point those cities had some special authority, but because those Christian communities retained living memory of the proclamation of the apostles themselves, and this memory verified that these were the books they had received from those same apostles.

---

dependence on Mark. However, scattered references among the Fathers and other early Christian literature point to a preceding version of St. Matthew's Gospel, often described as being in Hebrew or Aramaic. But the Greek text of St. Matthew's Gospel shows little sign of being translated into Greek. This other text, then, may be a no longer extant Hebrew or Aramaic Gospel text also associated with St. Matthew. That text's relationship to our Matthew remains unclear.

5   *Against Heresies*, 3.1.1.
6   Ibid., 5.30.3.

This language will remain important for centuries, as the Fathers do not speak about which books wield some authority or show some sign of divine inspiration, but rather speak about the books they have received. It is also important to note that, even at this early date, the Gospel codices contain precisely these four, and this is true across the world. It is not the case that individual communities used individual Gospels and when they eventually came together, they combined the four. Nor do we have a single instance of any other Gospels being included in these codices. In fact, the earliest of the Gnostic gospels, the Gospel of Thomas, was being written in the early to mid-second century. It could not possibly have been included any more than those composed later could have been.

It is also now broadly accepted by scholars that by the year AD 100, St. Paul's Epistles had been gathered into a collection and were circulating together rather than as individual books. One of our earliest manuscripts of his Epistles is, in fact, an early edition of this collection, identified as Parchment 46. This collection includes the Epistle to the Hebrews, directly after the Epistle to the Romans, but that is a subject for another time. Very good historical evidence, much of it from the controversy with Marcion of Sinope at the dawn of the second century, shows that the codex of the Gospels and the codex of St. Paul's Epistles were already functioning as Scripture in Christian worship throughout the world in a way that's very similar to their function today in the Orthodox Church. In fact, 2 Peter 3:16 identifies St. Paul's Epistles collectively as Scripture.

This means that nineteen of the twenty-seven books were agreed upon as Scripture by all Christian communities during the earliest period in which we have historical evidence: the beginning of the second century. The other eight, then, the General (or Catholic) Epistles and the Revelation of St. John, are sometimes referred to as "disputed books," which gives the impression of debates about them ongoing for centuries. Again, however, this is a myth.[7] In the earliest centuries of the Church, no central or overarching authority structure existed beyond the local bishops in their cities. While bishops in various regions occasionally gathered in local councils to discuss pertinent issues, the findings of these councils exercised no authority or power over other bishops who were not involved.

We therefore have Christian communities developing across the Roman Empire and beyond who follow the teachings of the apostles on their own. This is what makes their early agreement on these nineteen books so stunning. But this development gets at what the word *canonical* means: a canonical text is one that exercises authority within a community. And these nineteen books held this authority in churches across the world. Individual churches then had additional books that exercised authority in their communities. As Christian communities came into contact, they evaluated each other as to whether they recognized each other as Christian or as something "other." One factor in these evaluations was the texts the other community used authoritatively. And so we see St. Irenaeus, in encountering Valentinian Gnostic communities, recognizing that they are not Christian churches like his own but rather something else, as they used a different set of texts and held a vastly different faith. On the other hand, when a community who had known only

---

7   This idea comes from a mistranslation of a distinction in Eusebius, who spoke of "*homolegoumena*," the books about which everyone says the same thing, and "*antilegomena*," books about which people say different things.

one Epistle of St. John encountered another that knew three, they recognized each other as Christian, despite this difference.

Of the remaining eight books—the seven General Epistles and the Revelation of St. John—some of them were accepted more widely than others and from an earlier date. The First Epistle of St. John was received universally by all who received his Gospel. Those groups who numbered a single epistle of St. John in the early centuries did so not because they rejected 2 and 3 John but because these letters were unknown to them. It is clear on even a cursory reading of the three Johannine epistles that they have the same author, and there is nothing in the brief 2 and 3 John that contradicts 1 John in any way.

First Peter was likewise widely accepted and uncontroversial in its authorship among communities who received it in the ancient Church. Second Peter and Jude are two closely related texts that appear to have circulated together and to have been collected with 1 Peter early in the second century, despite clear differences in the Greek between 1 and 2 Peter. The Fathers rarely cite the Epistle of St. James before the latter half of the second century, but there is no record of rejection among any Christian communities who knew the text. These seven texts were collected as the General Epistles and circulated as a unit by the end of the second century AD, as witnessed by St. Clement of Alexandria, who wrote a commentary on them as a unit.

The Revelation of St. John is a special case in that it was not only unknown but actively rejected by many Christian communities. In the third and fourth centuries, the adherence of certain schismatic groups, chiefly the Montanists, to belief in chiliasm (or millennialism) led to the Book of Revelation being considered part and parcel of their beliefs and therefore rejected by orthodox Christians. It was only in the fifth century AD in the West (due to the work of St. Jerome) and the sixth century in the East (due to the work of St. Andrew of Caesarea) that the Book of Revelation was finally widely received as part of the New Testament canon.[8]

The eventual canon of twenty-seven books that developed over time was therefore descriptive, not prescriptive. It listed the books that held authority in the churches that were recognized as Christian. Despite how late the Church received the Book of Revelation (and in the vast majority of churches, it is still not read liturgically), these churches acknowledge the shared faith of other Christian churches that did use the text of Revelation. We can, therefore, see that the only entity that chose the books that would comprise our New Testament is the Holy Spirit. The New Testament canon can be seen to have developed in the life of the Holy Spirit in the Church, the shared life of the Christian people, which the Orthodox Church calls Holy Tradition. It was neither the decision of certain authoritative men nor the recognition, based on a series of criteria, of a group of learned men. The Fathers treated as authoritative those texts they had received as authoritative, just as we do today.

---

8   The definitive source on the reception history of the Revelation of St. John is Eugenia Constantinou's *Guiding to a Blessed End: Andrew of Caesarea and His Apocalypse Commentary in the Ancient Church* (Catholic University of America Press, 2013).

CHAPTER THREE

How Did the Bible Get to Me?

F OR NEARLY TWO THOUSAND YEARS, the texts that make up the New Testament have been copied and recopied by Christians. Those of the Old Testament have been copied for even longer, by both Jewish and Christian scribes. Due to the oppressive policies of the Ottoman Empire, and despite the invention of the printing press in the sixteenth century, the first printed edition of the Greek New Testament in Greek-speaking Christian lands was not produced until 1904.[1] A printed edition of the Greek Old Testament took even longer. Hand-copied biblical texts were still being used in Greek churches well into the twentieth century. During this time and through human copying, variations entered the text. This led to the emergence of certain forms of the text in certain geographical areas at certain times. The study of this history—of copying the Scriptures and their subsequent variations—is called textual criticism.

---

1   This text was revised in 1912 and is often referred to as the Patriarchal text
     due to its commissioning by the Patriarch of Constantinople.

As mentioned with regard to inerrancy, it is important to understand that this is a process that occurred under the guidance of the Holy Spirit and within the Church. The texts with which we concern ourselves, primarily Greek texts, are manuscript copies made within the Orthodox Church and for the use of the Orthodox Church. A large percentage of our extant New Testament manuscripts are lectionary texts. These are literally the Gospel books that sat upon altars in Orthodox churches, as well as the epistle books that were read in the churches in centuries past. These are the texts that were copied and studied in Orthodox monasteries. Our biblical manuscripts, therefore, represent Holy Tradition, the life of the Holy Spirit in the Church, in its purest form.

This belief transforms the way in which Orthodox Christians practice textual criticism. In the past, textual criticism made its goal the establishment of an "original text." We have already shown why this is impossible. But academic textual criticism has become aware of this fact and has begun to reinterpret its end goal. The original text is a mirage. It appears from a distance but as one draws closer and closer to it, it disappears. An important evangelical Protestant statement on inerrancy[2] states that the "original text" is inspired and inerrant, and that text can now be established with a high degree of confidence using modern tools. This would, however, mean that for the vast majority of the history of the Church, she lacked an inspired and inerrant Bible.

The Orthodox belief that the Spirit guides the Church means that neither the first-century form of the text nor a modern

---

2   *The Chicago Statement on Inerrancy*, 1978.

reconstruction of that text can be privileged over the copies of the Scripture read and prayed within the Church for two millennia. Every generation of Christians, in every tribe and tongue and nation, has received the Scriptures that the Holy Spirit intended for them to have. We in our modern era have been uniquely blessed with a vast richness of biblical traditions from many times, places, and languages, due in no small part to our ability to use digital tools to compare and collate manuscripts, as well as the many manuscripts found over the past century. An Orthodox Christian participates in textual criticism, therefore, not to establish a hypothetical perfect or true text at the expense of all others. Rather, an Orthodox Christian participates in textual criticism to understand, appreciate, and learn from the vast wealth of traditions with which we have been blessed.

Old Testament Textual Criticism

TEXTUAL CRITICISM OF THE OLD and New Testaments actually represents two very different disciplines. The scribal discipline that copied and handed down the Hebrew text of the Old Testament was meticulous and produced an astounding achievement. Before the discovery of the Dead Sea Scrolls, the earliest text of the Hebrew Bible still extant dated from the beginning of the eleventh century. This manuscript is known as the Leningrad Codex (or Codex Leningradensis) and was named for the place of its discovery. This codex represents a text tradition called the Masoretic text, often abbreviated as MT. It is named for the Masoretes, the copyists responsible for this particular text tradition. The Masoretes not only copied the text with great precision and detail but added a significant number of textual and marginal notes. These include vowel markings that give pronunciations for reading the Hebrew text aloud. The text also includes notations for a daily and weekly cycle of reading the text for synagogues.

To aid in copying, the Masoretes placed markers for the middle points of verses and books. At the end of each book, a word count is given along with the first, middle, and last words of each book so that a copyist could verify the correctness of the copy.

This methodology was so successful for copying the Hebrew Bible that when the Dead Sea Scrolls were discovered, the match between texts was impressively accurate. In some cases, these texts written in the second century BC were nearly 100 percent identical to the previously oldest known text, from AD 1008. This means that textual criticism of the Old Testament is not so much about the history of changes in the shape of the Hebrew text; rather, it is based on comparing the Hebrew text of the Masoretic tradition, the MT, to other ancient texts in Hebrew, Aramaic, Greek, and other languages.

The Masoretic text was preserved with incredible accuracy from the time of the apostles to today. However, as shown conclusively by the Dead Sea Scrolls and other finds, several versions of biblical books and other textual traditions were extant in the first century AD. Additionally, many of the texts that now make up the Old Testament were still in flux at that time, and so translations such as the Greek sometimes reveal older Hebrew readings than those reflected in even our oldest Hebrew texts. Understanding these different strands of Old Testament textual tradition, their development, and how they came to hold authority in different Jewish and Christian communities is the discipline of Old Testament textual criticism.

The Greek Old Testament Tradition

IT IS COMMON IN BOTH popular and scholarly sources to shorthand the entire Greek Old Testament tradition as "the Septuagint." There are, however, a number of problems with this when we address the actual Greek text of the books of the Old Testament. The term *Septuagint* is a transliteration of the Latin word for "seventy." According to the *Letter of Aristeas*,[3] the translation of the Hebrew Scriptures into Greek began in the middle of the third century BC with the Torah, or Pentateuch. This translation was performed by seventy (or seventy-two) Jewish scribes in Alexandria, Egypt, who each translated the Torah over the course of seventy days. At the end of that time period, their translations all miraculously matched perfectly. When the Church Fathers refer to the "work of the Seventy," they are referring to this translation of the Pentateuch.

Strictly speaking then, the term "Septuagint" refers only to the first five books and not to an entire Old Testament. There is then no "Septuagint canon." Historically, following the translation of the Torah, other texts of the Hebrew Bible and other Jewish texts in general were translated into Greek. At least one text, the Book of Wisdom, which came to occupy a place in the Old Testament of the Orthodox Church, was originally written in Greek. These translations were not conducted by a central authority or by an organized group of scribes. They were done piecemeal and over the course of centuries. When these texts

---

3   The *Letter of Aristeas* is a letter dating to the early second century BC that describes the translation of the Torah or Pentateuch into Greek. It was widely regarded within Second Temple Judaism and early Christianity as an authoritative historical source.

are referred to collectively, they are more appropriately called the "Old Greek" rather than the Septuagint.

In addition to these early Greek translations, at least four further efforts were made to translate the Hebrew Scriptures into Greek. An unknown author or authors made one of these. This version, or recension, is known as the *kaige* recension. This name comes from a Greek transitional phrase used to begin sentences *kai ge* (roughly "and then"), which is used commonly throughout this version. Because the exact origin of this version is unknown, its time of composition is likewise subject to conjecture. But fragments have been found dating back to at least the first century AD. Early Jewish and Christian writers shed no real light on the origin of this version, as no references to it can be positively confirmed.

More established are the origins of the other three. The Old Greek translation of the Hebrew Scriptures had proved a remarkable success and had found acceptance in Jewish communities all over the world. This Greek translation was the only version of the Scriptures allowed to be read in the synagogue other than the original. Because Hebrew was virtually unknown in Jewish communities outside of Judea, the Scriptures were read in Greek in most synagogues of the Jewish diaspora, even in regions as close to Judea as Galilee. This is the primary reason that the Greek renderings of these texts are most commonly[4] quoted in the New Testament. As the vast majority of the texts that make up the New Testament were written to Christian

---

4   Roughly 70 percent of the Old Testament quotations in the New Testament come from the Old Greek.

communities outside of Judea, the authors quote the version of the text that was familiar to their hearers, both Jew and Gentile.

The early Christian use of the Greek Scriptures led to Jewish communities' rejection of them. Following the end of the Bar-Kokhba rebellion at the beginning of the second century AD, Jerusalem had been destroyed, and a new Roman city had been built over it. The Romans had expelled the entire Jewish community from the city. In the face of this, those Jewish communities that had not embraced Jesus as the Messiah reevaluated their community life and beliefs in order to form a way of life that could survive without a city or temple. The end result of this process was the religion we now know as Rabbinic Judaism. The definition of Judaism was narrowed, and the vast variety of beliefs that had been found in Second Temple Judaism was pruned. Christians were declared to be of a foreign religion and were expelled from the synagogues systematically.

Part of this reevaluation and retrenchment centered upon the Hebrew Scriptures and their canonical form. At this point these Jewish communities set limits and resolved which texts were in and which were out of what would be the Hebrew Bible. The wide array of Jewish texts that had flourished in Second Temple Judaism were pruned back to a core that would function authoritatively within Rabbinic Judaism. This core extended not only to the texts themselves but to translations and versions apart from what was decided to be the authoritative Hebrew textual tradition. This process did not immediately cause a change in Jewish communities' view of the reading of the Scriptures in the Greek language within the Greek synagogue. Rather, in the mid-second century AD, it took the form of new translations being made based on the Hebrew text that these Jewish communities now considered exclusively authoritative. Saint Justin the Philosopher and others alive at the time attest to this translation activity and the replacement of older, traditional Greek texts, which had been utilized by Christian communities, with new translations considered by Jewish communities to be more accurate.

The first and most immediately successful of these new translations was performed by Aquila of Sinope, a Jewish scholar who lived through the Bar-Kokhba rebellion at the beginning of the second century AD. Aquila had at one point become a Christian but returned to Judaism when he discovered that early Christian communities condemned the practice of astrology, which was then popular in the Jewish diaspora. It is likely his version that St. Justin argues against so vehemently in *Dialogue with Trypho*. Saint Jerome, however, writing at a later date past the time of controversy, considered Aquila's translation to be faithful to the point of being woodenly literal in its translation of the Hebrew text—which would become the Masoretic text—into Greek.

Symmachus, a Samaritan who had converted to join the Jewish community, undertook the second major translation effort in the mid-second century AD. Symmachus's approach was the opposite of Aquila's. His translation made rich use of Greek idioms and turns of phrase to convey the ideas and the beauty of the Hebrew text. While less technically accurate, this translation had a much higher literary quality in the Greek language and so became very popular among educated Greek readers.

Later in the second century AD, Theodotion, a Jewish scholar from the Greek-speaking Jewish diaspora, created yet another translation of the Hebrew Scriptures into Greek. Theodotion's version proved to hold little popularity within Jewish communities but attained a high level of popularity in Christian communities. In particular, Theodotion's version of the Book of Daniel, very different from that of the Old Greek in both style and content, displaced the Old Greek version in Christian usage. Only two manuscripts survive that contain the Old Greek version of Daniel. Every other existing manuscript of Daniel in Greek is based on Theodotion's translation, and it is this version from which the Orthodox Church reads liturgically on, for example, Holy Saturday.[5]

In the early third century AD, Origen produced the first major effort in the field of textual criticism. Known as the *Hexapla* because it was organized in six columns, this work placed in parallel the Hebrew text of the Old Testament, the Hebrew text transliterated into Greek characters, the Old Greek, Aquila's version, Symmachus's version, and Theodotion's version. The *Hexapla* became the standard means for studying the text of the Christian Old Testament for centuries thereafter. In addition to presenting the texts in parallel columns, Origen produced a system of critical markings, which he used to note differences between the texts and to draw scholars' attention to them. This basic methodology would go on to be used in critical texts of the Scriptures to this very day.

Following on and making use of Origen's work, two major Christian scholars edited the Old Testament in Greek during the latter half of the third century for use in Christian churches. One of these versions was prepared by St. Lucian of Antioch,

---

5   This means that the version of Daniel that is canonical in the Orthodox Church was produced by a non-Christian Jewish scholar in the second century AD.

a scholar trained in Edessa, Syria, who was later entangled in charges of heresy at the time of the condemnation of Paul of Samosata. He was later reconciled to the Church and ended his life in martyrdom. His edited text of the Greek Old Testament was used by most of the fourth- and fifth-century Church Fathers, notably St. John Chrysostom. Another similar Christian Old Testament was produced through the editorial work of St. Hesychius, an Egyptian bishop. Like St. Lucian, St. Hesychius was martyred under Domitian at the end of the third century. St. Hesychius's Greek version of the Old Testament was used throughout Egypt until the Fourth Ecumenical Council.

All the work on the text described above took place before our oldest complete copies of the Christian Old Testament in Greek. These manuscripts were then copied and recopied through the centuries until the beginning of the twentieth century in the Greek-speaking Christian world. Christian scribes and copyists did not practice the same rigorous disciplines of their Jewish counterparts who copied the Hebrew text. As we will also see in the case of the New Testament, this reality has produced a great degree of variation within the text of the Greek Old Testament. This gives us a rich tradition, but it also means that it is impossible to speak of "the Greek Old Testament" or the Septuagint as a single text. Though many modern scholarly works will still reference the Septuagint in their titles, this is done with the understanding that the term is really serving as a handy label for a variety of texts from across the Christian centuries.

Again, it is incorrect to say that the Septuagint is the Orthodox Old Testament. In discussing the formation of the Old Testament canon, not all Orthodox churches have received the same set of Old Testament texts. But even within the Greek Old

Testament tradition, a great deal of variation exists. The manuscripts of the Greek Old Testament that have survived to this day are Orthodox Christian Old Testaments. Many of the oldest manuscripts come from ancient Orthodox monastic foundations, with Codex Sinaiticus, discovered at St. Catherine's Monastery, serving as Exhibit A of this fact.

Though the Greek Old Testament tradition is a translation tradition, this does not mean that it always represents a later stage of the text than the Hebrew. A large number of Greek Old Testament manuscripts, even complete Christian Old Testaments in Greek, predate the Masoretic text by centuries. Critics often countered this argument in the past by pointing to the superior precision exercised by Jewish scribes and copyists when compared to those in Christian communities. However, more recent textual finds, especially the Dead Sea Scrolls discussed below, have revealed that in the vast majority of cases where there is a clear variation between Greek Old Testament texts and the Masoretic Text, the Greek is actually translating a different, sometimes older Hebrew text. This has led scholars of all backgrounds to the conclusion that the Greek texts are not an inferior witness to a single Hebrew scriptural text tradition, but rather a unique witness to another part of that text tradition that is of at least equal antiquity.

The Aramaic Old Testament

THE TARGUMS

THE PERSIAN EMPEROR CYRUS THE Great allowed the Jewish exiles in Babylon to return to what became the Persian province of Judea circa 516 BC. The language used throughout the expanding Persian Empire was Aramaic, a Semitic language that is roughly a cousin to biblical Hebrew and other Semitic dialects. Though the exile had lasted only seventy years, by the time of the return, the vast majority of the Jewish people could not read or understand Hebrew. We see this in Ezra's need to accompany the reading of the Torah with an Aramaic translation (2 Ezra/ Nehemiah 8:7–8). Several Old Testament texts written after the exile, such as Ezra and Daniel, have major portions written in Aramaic. Further, the Hebrew Old Testament as it presently exists is written not in Hebrew lettering but in Aramaic block letters, and during that revision, Aramaic words and phrases found their way into many parts of the Old Testament text.

To answer the need for the availability of the Hebrew Scriptures in Aramaic, scribes made translations that became known as Targums. These translations, however, were not translations in the modern sense but rather expanded versions of the scriptural text that included additional traditions and interpretations. The Targums are, in a sense, like a study Bible in which the notes have been incorporated into the main text without distinction. This made the Scriptures and their accompanying traditions more available to the Jewish people of the Persian era. The scribal class was aware of the deviations of the Targums from the original Hebrew texts, so they could only be read in synagogues if the Hebrew had been read first. The Targums, therefore, were never accorded the same status that Jewish scholars and teachers accorded to the later Greek translations of the Hebrew Scriptures.

These Aramaic versions are known as Targums, plural, because there are a great number of them. Five of these have been identified from literary remains, but fragments of many more unidentified Targums have been discovered at synagogues in Egypt. The Targums provide a valuable witness not only to an early stage of the text of the Hebrew Scriptures, but also to how those texts were interpreted and understood in Jewish communities in the late centuries BC and the early centuries AD. This style of commenting on the text by adding information would later develop into the Jewish commentary style of Midrash. A number of these interpretations find their way into the New Testament in various places, as the New Testament authors shared the traditions surrounding the Hebrew Scriptures that were codified in the Targums. Their very existence demonstrates that for Jewish believers of the first century AD, the exact line dividing the text itself from the interpretive tradition handed down over generations was blurry at best and, in many cases, virtually nonexistent.

THE SAMARITAN PENTATEUCH

THE SAMARITANS DERIVE THEIR NAME from the region surrounding what was once the city of Samaria, the capital of the Northern Kingdom of Israel before its destruction by the Assyrians. In order to prevent insurrection, the Assyrians frequently deported conquered peoples and then resettled their lands with people from other parts of their empire. While people might be willing to take up arms to retake their ancestral lands, tenant farmers from elsewhere were less likely to be so inspired. This happened to Israel, and those Israelites who remained following the Assyrian deportations intermarried with the new arrivals, producing a group of people who were part Jewish in heritage and part Gentile. This group came to have its own religious practices, divergent from those of Judah and later Judea. These centered around a temple built on Mt. Gerizim near present-day Nablus until the destruction of that temple circa 150 BC by the Judean king John Hyrcanus.

In addition to the traditional practices that ethnic Samaritans have maintained in Palestine to this day, the Samaritans have their own textual tradition of the Torah. This text is today referred to as the Samaritan Pentateuch and was known by the Church Fathers as the *Samaritikon*. Originally, this text was written in the Samaritan dialect, a Semitic language closely related to Hebrew but with its own written alphabet. Eventually, for the same reasons described above, the Samaritan Pentateuch was translated into Aramaic and even had at least one Targum written by a certain Nathanael.[6]

The Samaritan Pentateuch is important for textual criticism of the Old Testament for two primary reasons. First, there are thousands of small differences in readings between the Torah as represented by the Samaritans and the Hebrew Torah represented in the Masoretic text. Manuscripts of the Samaritan Pentateuch in many cases vastly predate the Masoretic text, making them an important early witness to the text of the Torah. Some of these variations are directly related to the Samaritan theological tradition. The most classic example of such a variation occurs in Exodus 20:17 of the Samaritan Pentateuch, which, after the Ten Commandments, adds a command to construct

---

6   While a Samaritan community still exists today, the vast majority of the Samaritan communities of the turn of the era ended up becoming Christian or later converting to Islam. Nablus itself, then Neapolis, was a Christian village from at least the early part of the second century AD, for example.

the temple at Mt. Gerizim. These variations, which are obvious amendments of the text to favor the Samaritan point of view, represent a tiny minority of the textual variants involved.

In the second place, a majority of the nonsectarian variants between the Samaritan and Masoretic texts are held in common with the Septuagint. The Samaritan Pentateuch, therefore, lends additional evidence to the antiquity of many of the Septuagint readings.

THE SYRIAC OLD TESTAMENT

SYRIAC IS A LANGUAGE THAT developed originally as a dialect of Aramaic used in the area around Edessa in Syria. While linguistically a form of Aramaic, it is written in cursive scripts that more closely resemble Arabic, which evolved out of Syriac centuries later. Edessa became a major hub of Christianity and of Christian learning in the second, third, and fourth centuries AD, so the Syriac Old Testament, which developed from Babylonian Jewish traditions, became an important text. A number of early saints came out of this Syriac tradition, most notably St. Ephraim the Syrian, whose hymns are rich in Syriac Old Testament allusion and commentary.

The Syriac Old Testament was translated directly from the Hebrew text at some point in the early first century AD by the Jewish community in and around Edessa. It therefore gives a witness to the state of the Hebrew text as held by Babylonian Jewish communities, which remained in Mesopotamia after the return of many of the exiles to Judea under Cyrus. This provides a standard for comparison with the Masoretic text, which represents the preservation of a Palestinian line of the textual tradition. A translation of the New Testament into Syriac from the Greek was added to this existing Old Testament translation to form a Syriac Bible. This Syriac Bible was used by the aforementioned saints and Christian scholars until the early seventh century, circa AD 616, when the whole text, both Old and New Testaments, was revised to more closely match the then current Greek text. This means that only manuscripts that predate the seventh century are useful as independent witnesses to the Old Testament text.

The Dead Sea Scrolls

AS MENTIONED EARLIER, THE DEAD Sea Scrolls represent the most significant textual discovery of modern times. Their discovery transformed scholarly understanding of the text of the Old Testament and opened up the wealth and richness of the tradition of the Hebrew Scriptures. Additionally, the insights into the community at Qumran, which produced these scrolls, has transformed our understanding of the nature of Jewish and early Christian communities in the period of Christian origins, shedding further light on both the formation of the Christian Old Testament and the composition of the New Testament. What's more, this is an ongoing find: a twelfth cave was discovered in 2017.

Between 1946 and 1956, eleven caves were discovered in Wadi Qumran[7] that contained scrolls stored inside clay jars. Qumran lies near the Dead Sea and at a low elevation. The subsequently dry climate served to preserve these texts for nearly two millennia.

---

7   A wadi is a riverbed that floods during periods of high rain.

The scrolls were produced by a Jewish community at Qumran who lived in relative isolation between the second century BC and the first century AD, at which point Roman military action destroyed the community. Before this destruction, however, the people stored their priceless scrolls in the caves, likely in hopes that survivors might someday return to recover them.

The vast majority of the scrolls, roughly 90 percent, were written on sheets of sheepskin vellum that were sewn together. The remainder were written on papyrus, a sort of early paper made from pressed reeds. The black ink came from the soot produced by olive oil lamps, and sharpened reeds served as pens. After the scrolls were stored within the pottery jars, the jars were sealed with wax and then placed in their respective caves.

Found among the Dead Sea Scrolls were copies of a large number of Old Testament texts. In many cases, multiple copies of the same text were discovered, and sometimes multiple versions of the same text, as was the case with the Book of Jeremiah. All the books of the Masoretic text were present at Qumran except for Esther. Additionally, archaeologists found a calendar that was used by the community in its cycle of fasts and feasts. Notably, Purim was not included in it, implying that Esther as a whole was absent from the Qumran community's tradition. The books of Tobit and Ben Sirach/Ecclesiasticus were stored in quantity, as were the Epistle of Jeremiah and Psalm 151. Significant quantities of the books of 1 Enoch and Jubilees were also stored in the caves.[8] A wide variety of texts peculiar to the community, its founder, its daily life, and its specific religious

---

8   In fact, more copies of 1 Enoch and Jubilees were found at Qumran than copies of Genesis or Exodus.

teachings were found, which are unknown outside of Qumran. The texts are in a variety of languages, including several dialects of Hebrew and Aramaic as well as Greek.

The Dead Sea Scrolls have given us access to manuscripts from the Masoretic text tradition written more than one thousand years before the earliest previously known manuscripts. This has allowed us to assess the level to which Jewish scribes and copyists were able to maintain the integrity of that text over time. Further, the scrolls have given us access to other Hebrew textual traditions of the ancient world, most notably those manuscripts that formed the basis for the Septuagint and the other Old Greek translations. They have given us a window into the process of canon formation in individual communities parallel to the way in which this process took place in the early Christian communities. They also have given us a firsthand witness to the wide variation of Jewish belief and practice in the period in which Christianity emerged, and that gives us a greater understanding of how Christian communities existed and lived within the world of Second Temple Judaism. This last point, critically, transformed the scholarly consensus about the way many of the texts that came to make up the New Testament were read.

New Testament Textual Criticism

NEW TESTAMENT TEXTUAL CRITICISM IS functionally a very different discipline from Old Testament textual criticism. A massive number of manuscripts in the original language (Greek), going back to the middle part of the second century AD, attest to the New Testament text. In many cases, the earliest known manuscripts of New Testament texts date to within fifty to one hundred years of their composition. This is a stark contrast with the Old Testament, where often the earliest known manuscripts date to centuries or even a millennium after their original composition and are in a language different from the one in which they were originally composed. Further, the Greek manuscripts of the New Testament come from a wide variety of locations and traditions scattered all over the former Roman world. Our earliest Old Testament manuscripts all come from one location, Qumran, and represent in most cases multiple copies of the same text.

As mentioned previously, the earliest phases of modern textual criticism were focused on attempting to get as close as possible to a hypothetical "original text," although we've established that this text is difficult to identify. Due to the nature of the texts available to us, however, a sort of impenetrable fog covers the second quarter of the second century AD. It is extremely doubtful, for practical reasons, that any New Testament texts will be found that predate this barrier. In some cases, as with Luke-Acts, two versions of texts both disappear into this barrier with no objective means to judge their relationship. This has led the discipline to refocus on describing the various shapes and traditions of the New Testament text as a historical matter and abandon its quixotic quest for "the original."

The extant manuscripts of the New Testament text come in several types and present a variety of features that largely depend upon their date of composition. Additionally, variation in format exists based on the region of their provenance. That the copying of these manuscripts took place across such a diverse range of places and times is positive evidence of the preservation of the New Testament text. There was never a time in the history of the Church, despite certain conspiracy theories, in which one central authority had control over the Greek text of the New Testament. This means that at no point in time could the text have been systematically altered or corrupted at the behest of some individual or group. An alteration of the text in one place at one time could be countered by copies of the text from earlier times and other places.

This was precisely the method taken by the Church Fathers in correcting the errors of heretics such as Marcion who argued from their own versions of New Testament texts. While over two millennia, thousands of small variations between manuscripts have appeared, the sheer number of diverse manuscript traditions allows these variations to be identified as such and easily dealt with. Whether a variant is as simple as a spelling error or omitted word on the one hand, or a deliberate change of the text on the other, manuscripts of the text are available to make the correction. In no place in the New Testament are significant elements of the text ambiguous or lost.

The New Testament Manuscripts

AT THE TIME OF THIS writing, just over 5,800 New Testament manuscripts exist. The majority of these are not New Testament manuscripts in the sense that they are copies of the entire New Testament, but in that they represent manuscripts of New Testament material. The earliest of these is a credit card–sized papyrus fragment of the Gospel of John dated to around AD 125. This means that our manuscript evidence begins roughly thirty years after the composition of the document that it represents. Our manuscripts of other New Testament books commence shortly thereafter, in the middle part of the second century. The gap for other books is larger than that for St. John's Gospel, which was one of the latest books written despite possessing the earliest manuscript evidence. The longest gap is around one hundred years. For most New Testament books, it is somewhere around seventy-five years.

This vast number of manuscript sources is particularly striking when compared to other Greek and Latin literature from the ancient world. For example, we know of Aristotle's commentary *Constitution of Athens* from four Greek manuscripts. None of these manuscripts is complete, and even when all four are collated, gaps are present in the text. We know of Thucydides' *History of the Peloponnesian War*, written in the fifth century BC, from eight manuscripts, the earliest from around AD 900. This represents a gap of more than thirteen hundred years. Julius Caesar's account *The Gallic Wars* is known from ten manuscripts, the earliest of which dates to the ninth century AD, representing a gap of nine hundred years. Tacitus's *The Annals and the Histories* is an important historical work regarding the Roman Empire that includes some of the earliest information about the origins of Christianity. It was written around AD 100 in thirty books, only fourteen of which, plus portions of another three, still exist. The surviving books are known in only two extant manuscripts that date to the ninth century and the eleventh century respectively.

With literally thousands of handwritten copies, obviously any given New Testament manuscript will contain variations and outright errors. There are many suggestions as to why this is so. Most likely it is because, for most of its history in most of the world, Christianity was not a primarily text-based religion. The focus of Christianity was the liturgical celebration of the Eucharist and the moral life. This is not to say that the text of Scripture was irrelevant, but rather that the public reading and preaching of Scripture served these other two ends. The Scriptures were preached to build up believers in their lives of virtue and prayer, and the reading of Scripture was a central liturgical and ritual act in the Eucharistic gathering. In contrast, following the destruction of the temple in Jerusalem in AD 70, Rabbinic Judaism lost the vast majority of its ritual life, with the text of the Hebrew Bible as its only artifact of what Judaism had been.

This meant that for Christian scribes, the absolute preservation of every detail of the text was less imperative. It was also not considered a major problem when notes, known as "glosses," on commonly held interpretations of confusing parts of the text crept into the text itself. While the cycle of readings in the Hebrew Bible is denoted in the vast majority of ancient manuscripts with small notations in the carefully preserved text, Christians of all eras felt very free to divide and rearrange the New Testament text in lectionaries. In these readings, they also felt free to add introductory and concluding words to the readings and to sometimes leave out sentences or whole paragraphs for the purpose of constructing a cohesive single story.

A common argument of New Testament textual skeptics is that there are more variations between the manuscripts of the New Testament than there are words in the New Testament. This argument is made in an attempt to create a sort of pessimism about the text of the New Testament, as if there are so many variations and copying mistakes that it is impossible to determine what the text was originally meant to say. Enough has been said already on the quest for "the original." But it deserves also to be said that these same critics, when pressed, will admit that only a handful of these variations and mistakes make any difference whatsoever to the understanding of the text. The vast majority are simple misspellings that are easily corrected by the thousands of other extant copies and knowledge of the Greek language. Even in the case of that handful of variants that actually alter the meaning, none touch any point of Christian doctrine whatsoever. While there can be a great deal of disagreement about what the New Testament means, what it says is an objective reality. And this is true not only in our time with our wealth of manuscripts and computer tools, but for every era of the Church.

Of these 5,800 manuscripts, between 40 and 45 percent are lectionary manuscripts, which have been largely neglected in the study of the New Testament text and its history. This omission has occurred for various reasons, the chief being that the text of any given book in a lectionary is presented in a fragmentary manner and out of order, with words and phrases introducing and concluding those readings. Comparing such a manuscript to another manuscript, whether of another lectionary or a non-lectionary text, can be extremely difficult. The primary version of the critical Greek text of the New Testament, which is printed on the main pages (as opposed to the notes) of a Greek text that can be purchased today, takes into account only two lectionary manuscripts out of thousands. In contrast, the Patriarchal text of 1904–12 is compiled from 250 lectionary manuscripts dating from between the ninth and fifteenth centuries AD. It, therefore, represents the only significant source of information on the text of the lectionaries that were actually read liturgically in Greek-speaking churches through history. Even this text, however, utilizes only a fraction of the available information.

Modern Greek New Testaments utilize the other segment of manuscripts, in which the books of the New Testament are written in their entirety. But even these manuscripts are often not complete New Testaments. In the vast majority of cases, they are manuscripts of either the Gospels or the Epistles, as the Scriptures are still used liturgically in the Orthodox Church. These two books, traditionally called in Greek the *Evangelikon* and *Apostolikon*, stem from the very early collections of New Testament texts that we previously discussed with regard to the formation of the New Testament canon.

Families of Manuscripts

THOUGH THE PRACTICE HAS RECENTLY fallen out of favor, it was once traditional in the field of textual criticism to speak about "families" of New Testament manuscripts. As manuscripts were discovered, studied, and catalogued, patterns started to emerge: certain variations in the text would appear in more than one manuscript. The best explanation for these matches was that these manuscripts were somehow related. For example, one might be a copy of the other, or they both may have been copied from the same original manuscript. This includes both regular variations and mistakes. As these patterns began to emerge between manuscripts, scholars noted that, very broadly, many of these correlations also corresponded to the rough geographic area and time period from which these manuscripts came. In order to speak about these manuscripts as groups, as collections of texts with similar characteristics, they were labeled as being certain "text types" or "text families."

ALEXANDRIAN TYPE

THE EARLIEST OF THESE TEXT types is the Alexandrian, representing manuscripts found primarily in Egypt and other parts of North Africa. The early date is the product once again of Egypt's climate, which has well preserved the material of early manuscripts, both papyrus and parchment. These manuscripts generally date to between the second and fourth centuries. After the fourth century, multiple factors caused the cessation of the copying of these manuscripts. The schism that occurred surrounding the Fourth Ecumenical Council led to the greater part of the Egyptian Church narrowing its focus to the Coptic biblical tradition and largely abandoning the Greek. The Islamic invasion of Egypt reinforced this practice, as Greek was viewed as a means of influence by the enemy Byzantine Empire.

These manuscripts, however, were Orthodox Bibles at the time of their production. They provide an important window into the biblical text during a foundational period in the Church's history and in an extremely vital portion of the Church in Alexandria. Largely because of the manuscripts' age and therefore relative uniformity, Westcott and Hort, the two most important textual critics in the formation of the modern Greek New Testament, labeled the Alexandrian text the "neutral text." In most modern Greek New Testaments, it constitutes the main body of the text, with variations and other text types reflected in the notes.

The Codex Sinaiticus is likely the most famous manuscript from the Alexandrian text family. It originally contained both Old and New Testaments in Greek, though most of the first half of the Old Testament is now lost. The New Testament is present in its entirety, and the Epistle of Barnabas and the Shepherd of Hermas are added to the end. The extant Old Testament text includes the books of Tobit, Judith, 1—4 Maccabees, and 4 Ezra. It is written on calfskin and was first copied in the fourth century. It is not, however, the product of a single scribe copying the entire biblical text. In the portions that still exist, there are at least three original copyists. In addition, a number of later hands have come in to correct or repair faded portions of the text. At least three of these correctors have been identified. It is referred to in scholarly literature with the Hebrew letter aleph.

Codex Sinaiticus was discovered by Constantin von Tischendorf, who traveled to St. Catherine's Monastery in the 1840s. Though there is a popular urban legend about the finding of the manuscript—specifically that it was in a trash pile or about to be burned—this is not the case. Rather, a monk showed Tischendorf the main body of the text, which was still held together. The monk had kept it in his cell, wrapped in a communion cloth as something precious. Tischendorf then searched the monastery in order to find missing leaves, a few of which he discovered with other damaged manuscripts that were going to be disposed of by burning. Once he had collected the other leaves he could find, he asked to take the codex with him. The monks declined, allowing him to take only a few pages.

Tischendorf returned to the monastery several years later under the patronage of Tsar Alexander II. In the meantime, several more leaves had been discovered. Tischendorf negotiated for all the known elements of the text to be presented to the tsar and, in return, Alexander II made substantial donations to both St. Catherine's and the monastery at Mt. Tabor. Additional leaves have been found sporadically over time. Most recently, several were uncovered during monastery renovations in 1975. The text of Codex Sinaiticus remained in the Russian National Library until 1933, when the Soviet government sold it to the British Museum for the equivalent of ten million dollars. The entirety of the currently known text has been scanned in high definition and is available online.[9]

Two other manuscripts of the Alexandrian text type are worthy of note. First is the manuscript known as Codex Vaticanus, named for the Vatican, where it has been since the fifteenth century. At the time that the text was brought to Rome, portions of Genesis, Kings/Kingdoms, and the final third of the New Testament were missing, and a copyist replaced them with new copies of the missing sections. Though it is debated, it is considered likely that Vaticanus is slightly older than Sinaiticus, dating back to the fourth century. It is indicated in scholarly literature with the letter "B." It is this particular Alexandrian manuscript which was copied to form the base text for modern Greek New Testaments.

The other major Alexandrian text is Codex Alexandrinus, which is abbreviated "A." Alexandrinus is named for spending most of its life in Alexandria before Patriarch of Constantinople Cyril Loukaris brought it to Constantinople in the sixteenth century. It was eventually given to the English monarchy and now resides in the British Museum. Alexandrinus dates to the

---

9   Codexsinaiticus.org.

fifth century AD and, of the three so far discussed, is the most complete and intact, with only minor damage to certain pages and sections.

WESTERN TEXT TYPE

THE SECOND MAJOR TEXT TYPE representing the New Testament is the Western text type, represented by relatively few manuscripts copied between the third and the ninth centuries AD. Already by the fifth and sixth centuries, very few scholars in the West were fluent in Greek, as Latin had become the dominant language. These are, however, the Greek texts that lie behind the New Testament of St. Jerome's Latin Vulgate. These manuscripts have a number of unique characteristics. In general, Western manuscripts are the freest in their copying of the texts, with many interpretations, elaborations, and even additional traditional details working their way directly into the text. In other manuscripts, these sorts of details are primarily confined to margins and introductions to books.

The version of Luke-Acts in the Western manuscripts, originally a two-volume work, is significantly longer than what appears in other types of manuscripts. The Book of the Acts of the Apostles, in particular, is 10 percent longer in the Western text than in other forms. Unlike most of the expansions in the Western text, many of the additional readings in St. Luke's Gospel are considered by scholars to be older than their omission in other texts. Which of the two versions of the Acts of the Apostles is older is the subject of a great deal of debate, with many scholars believing St. Luke himself wrote two versions, with one as a revision of the other.

The most significant manuscript of the Western text type is Codex Bezae. This text dates roughly to the year AD 400 and has been corrected by many hands during the intervening centuries. It was most likely copied in southern France or southern Italy, and it takes the form of two languages: Greek on one side and Latin on the other. While it was originally a complete New Testament, now only the Gospels, the Acts of the Apostles, and part of 3 John remain. The text receives its name from having come into the possession of the Protestant Reformer Theodore Beza in 1562 after being stolen by Huguenots. Beza donated the manuscript to Cambridge, where it remains to this day.

BYZANTINE TYPE

THE THIRD AND FINAL MAJOR text type is the Byzantine. Manuscripts of this type begin in the fifth century, not coincidentally with the collapse of the Western half of the Roman Empire. They continue until the early part of the twentieth century and the publication of the first printed Greek text by the Patriarch of Constantinople. These are the texts that were used throughout the Byzantine Empire during its history and by Greek-speaking Christians after the fall of Constantinople. Due to the fact that they are the more recent texts, more have survived. The Byzantine text type is represented in 80 percent of all currently known Greek manuscripts.

In recent years, the usefulness of these "text type" categories has been called into question. It is generally very difficult to make generalizations that function as hard and fast rules about New Testament manuscripts. The names of the families can also be quite misleading. For example, many of the Western manuscripts were discovered in Syria. Codex Washingtonianus was copied in Egypt. One of the correctors of Codex Alexandrinus was attempting to correct it to the Byzantine text type.

Generalizations may usually be true, but in specific cases, they often prove to be false. As researchers implement modern computer tools for scanning and collating manuscripts, we are discovering just how complex the relationships truly are between our thousands of manuscripts. People and the texts they carried with them were far more mobile in the ancient world than is often appreciated. Many texts which appear to be "hybrids" or unclassifiable according to the text-type system are now having their origins clarified through the reconstruction of their historical influences. Nevertheless, the terminology is still commonly used and should be understood.

Other Sources

THOUGH THE SITUATION OF THE New Testament is very different from that of the Old, ancient translations of the New Testament into other languages in the early Church are also useful in textual criticism. The biblical text was translated into Coptic, Syriac, and Armenian well before the schism surrounding the Fourth Ecumenical Council. The text was later translated into Latin piecemeal and then as a whole by St. Jerome. Later still, the text was translated into Georgian, and through Georgian into Slavonic. While none of these ancient versions gives us a direct witness to the wording of the Greek text, the translation was performed at a date earlier than many of our manuscripts. This means that these texts in other languages are pointers to the state of the Greek original at the time of translation. Additionally, these translations give clues as to how specific Greek words and phrases were understood at the time of translation.

Finally, the writings of the Church Fathers represent a wealth of resources with regard to the ancient form of the text. The writings of the Fathers are replete with quotations from the Scriptures in general and the New Testament in particular. These quotations give us a glimpse of what the text looked like when that Father was reading it. Certain Fathers quote the New Testament so extensively that scholars have been able to reconstruct most of their New Testament by linking together their quotations. As important as this evidence is, however, there are a few caveats.

It can sometimes be difficult to know how directly a particular Father is quoting a text. For example, when St. John Chrysostom cites a text in a homily, is he necessarily quoting it word for word, or might he be slightly paraphrasing in order to apply the text to his audience and purpose? For example, might he change a "they" to a "you" in order to hammer the point home to his listeners? Also, the works of the Church Fathers themselves have a manuscript history, and it is not as rich with copies as the text of the New Testament. It is difficult to be absolutely certain about a Father's exact wording. There are many cases where it appears that a copyist might have "corrected" a biblical quotation by making it match the copyist's version of the Bible.

All these sources allow access to the depth and riches of the biblical tradition, as these manuscripts represent just that: a tradition. The preservation of the text of the Scriptures is the work of the Holy Spirit in the Church. To attempt to identify some part of this tradition as "correct" or "right" or "pure" as opposed to the rest may be attractive in its simplicity, but it cuts such a person off from much of what the Holy Spirit has done in the Church. For Orthodox Christians, all these manuscripts represent a part of our shared scriptural heritage, and their study increases our appreciation of that heritage.

CHAPTER FOUR

Which Bible Should I Read?

T HE VAST MAJORITY OF ENGLISH-SPEAKING Ortho-
dox Christians will not be able to invest the time required
to master Greek, Aramaic, and Hebrew in order to read the biblical texts in their original languages. Even most members of the
clergy struggle to gain and maintain reading mastery of these
languages because of the demands on their time. For most people then, reading the Scriptures for purposes of worship, devo-
tion, study, and spiritual growth will take place through English
translations of the Bible.

Over the last several decades, the publication of various
Bibles has become a major industry in the United States and
other English-speaking nations. There are a great many translations, versions, formats, and study Bibles for nearly every age
and niche group. Dozens of versions of the Scriptures are available instantly online. Copyright law has led every major Christian press to produce its own translation or series of translations
of the Bible so that it can cite the translation(s) in its other published materials without royalty concerns. That means there are
many, many options when it comes to Bibles. Even a cursory

visit to the Bible section of a secular bookstore reveals just how overwhelming the decision can be for an Orthodox Christian in search of the right text to read and rely upon.

Every translation is an interpretation. There is a tendency to think, based on experience with dictionaries, that a word in one language "equals" a word in another language, such that all languages essentially parallel one another. This, however, is simply not the case, especially when speaking about ancient languages in comparison to a modern language. In Hebrew, for example, there is no system of verb tenses parallel to those in the English language. In classical Greek, there is no indefinite article ("a," "an"), and what is called the definite article in Greek ("the") is actually more of a demonstrative pronoun ("this," "that"). Countless other examples are possible.

In reality, languages have words that describe things, actions, and concepts. To understand a language means that by hearing or reading that language, you accurately understand the things, actions, and concepts to which the author or speaker is referring. To make a translation, therefore, one must both understand the original language in the sense of grasping the concepts being communicated and then be able to communicate accurately those same concepts in the other language. This is simple when translating something that is relatively static, such as "the brown horse." It can be much more complex, however, in other scenarios. For example, the primary element that determines the form of English verbs is time. Did the action happen in the past? Will it happen in the future? Is it happening right now? Hebrew and Aramaic verbs, however, do not communicate time at all. Greek verb forms likewise do not primarily refer to time. This means that to translate them into English requires a certain amount of subjective interpretation based upon context and other considerations.

Study Bibles generally identify themselves in terms of the perspective from which their notes are written. Many study Bibles identify themselves in their titles with a particular theological perspective, such as the *Orthodox Study Bible*, various Reformed study Bibles, Roman Catholic study Bibles, Lutheran study Bibles, and so on. Some study Bibles bear the name of a particular teacher or ministry. Others say they are aimed at a particular group, such as men, women, or children of a certain age. These identifiers make known the perspectives and biases that may exist in the study notes and other supplementary material. However, due to the nature of translation, these biases and perspectives exist within the actual text of the biblical version, not only in the notes. These subjective elements of the text are very rarely labeled clearly on Bibles for sale.

The purpose of this chapter, then, is to discuss first the various methodologies that are used in the translation of the biblical text. English Bibles can be grouped into categories based on these different approaches to translation. The first important factor to understand in selecting a Bible is the degree to which this particular version is attempting to reflect the original text or to provide a particular interpretation of it. This chapter will then discuss the history and methodology of a number of major popular English translations and their relative value for Orthodox Christians who are interested in reading the Scriptures for themselves. In this respect, the list will be in no way exhaustive, as new versions and revisions go in and out of print with regularity. Rather, it will describe the major traditions or families of

English Bible translations that Orthodox Christians will most commonly encounter.

Different Base Texts

BEFORE DISCUSSING DIFFERENT METHODS OF translating the Scriptures, it is important to outline the fact that differing English translations of the Bible are translated from different texts in the original languages. As discussed in the previous chapter, both Old and New Testaments are represented in a variety of manuscripts, versions, languages, and traditions. Before a translation can begin, scholars must select which text to translate. Different translators and translation boards have made different decisions in this respect. Even when a given translation attempts to be thorough in its notes regarding variations, translators still must choose which text will take center stage, as it were, on the page.

In the case of the Old Testament in English, relatively few options exist with regard to the base text. Nearly all English Bibles translate the Old Testament from the Masoretic text. For books that are not contained in the Masoretic text (because they are not a part of the Rabbinic Jewish canon), scholars translate them from the critical edition of the Greek text, primarily taken from Codex Vaticanus. They fill in gaps in a particular book or portion of the text from Sinaiticus or Alexandrinus. There is therefore very little difference in the vast majority of English Old Testaments with regard to the text being translated. These translations will, to varying degrees, reflect the readings of other manuscripts and text traditions in their notes.

The exceptions to this rule are English translations of the Greek Old Testament tradition, often labeled as translations of the Septuagint. We have already discussed the reasons why this identifier is problematic. Translators currently have only four real options in this regard in English.

First, Lancelot Breton prepared a rough translation of the Greek for the margin of his published Greek text. This translation is now in the public domain and is therefore often found online and in print, independent of the Greek original. This text can be difficult to read, as Breton chose to translate into English that parallels the King James Version (KJV), meaning that he wrote in a deliberately antiquated style. His text was also originally intended to accompany the Greek and serve as an aid to its understanding, not to stand on its own.

The most readable Old Testament based on the Greek tradition is the *Orthodox Study Bible*. The OSB follows traditional formatting of the text, albeit with the divisions used in the Greek text, giving it a familiarity that other Greek Old Testament translations lack. If this Bible's Old Testament has a drawback, it is inconsistency: Different individuals translated each book, so the translation strategy is not identical across all of the text. Likewise, the frequency and depth of the textual notes vary from book to book. Though it is the most readable text, it is not the best text for a more in-depth study of the Greek Old Testament in English.

The best text for the study of the Greek Old Testament in English is the New English Translation of the Septuagint, produced by the International Organization for Septuagint and Cognate Studies (IOSCS) and published by the Society for Biblical Literature, the scholarly guild for biblical studies. This edition has copious notes and introductions to each book discussing the text, the manuscripts, and their history. Where there are multiple versions of a book in Greek that differ greatly, these are translated in parallel columns for comparison. The translation is made for literal precision, however, over readability. While it is excellent for learning more about the Greek Old Testament tradition, it is not ideal for personal devotional use and general reading.

The most recent English translation of the Greek Old Testament tradition is the Lexham English Septuagint. Lexham Press is the print division of FaithLife, the company that produces Logos Bible Software. The Lexham English Septuagint aims to split the difference on readability and scholarly accuracy between the *Orthodox Study Bible* and the New English Translation of the Septuagint. In this respect, it mostly succeeds. The chief critique of the Lexham Septuagint is the selection of Greek text for translation. Essentially, the Lexham scholars have translated almost everything that was in one version of the published Greek text, H.B. Swete's *The Old Testament in English: According to the Septuagint.* Swete, in turn, included everything in the Codex Vaticanus. This means that the text includes not only 4 Maccabees and the Psalms of Solomon, but a particular (short) Greek version of 1 Enoch. It also includes the liturgical section of the codex, meaning that it features the nine biblical odes (with the ninth, the Magnificat, removed) as used in the Orthros or Matins services of the Orthodox Church. At the end of that section is a translation of what Orthodox readers will recognize as the Great Doxology, though translated in a way that clearly does not recognize its liturgical use.

In many cases, the precise text used for translation is historically conditioned, and this represents the greatest cause of variation. More simply put, the more recent a translation is, the more likely it is to take the latest manuscript discoveries into account. This is true in the case of the Old Testament regarding the Dead Sea Scrolls. It is even truer in the case of the New Testament, where the availability of manuscripts increased exponentially since the time the first printed Greek texts appeared in the West in the sixteenth century. This difference is responsible for the sometimes major and significant differences between the King James Version and modern translations, for example.

Every major English translation of the New Testament, including the King James Version, is based on what is called an "eclectic text." This means that, rather than using a single Greek source, several Greek manuscripts are used and brought together to form the Greek text to be translated. In each case, the translators sought the best manuscripts available before translating, although these varied over time. When Erasmus first published his printed Greek New Testament, he had only eight manuscripts to work from. He had three manuscripts of the Gospels, four manuscripts of the Epistles, and only one manuscript of the Book of Revelation. Further, his manuscript of the Book of Revelation was missing the ending, and so Erasmus created his own Greek version by translating the then available Latin version of Revelation backward into Greek.

The edition of the Greek New Testament from which the first English translations were made has become known as the *Textus Receptus*, or the "received text." This term is sometimes vaguely used to refer not only to Erasmus's text but also to other, later editions of the Greek New Testament that use manuscripts from the Byzantine type. Properly speaking, it refers to the four editions of the Greek New Testament published by Robertus Stephanus from 1546 to 1551. He produced these by editing and collating additional manuscripts with Erasmus's edition. Specifically, Stephanus brought thirteen other manuscripts or editions to bear, including the Codex Bezae, a Western manuscript. It was in the final edition of 1551 that Stephanus first added the now familiar chapter and verse divisions to the New Testament.

Another term used, and sometimes confused, with Textus Receptus is "the Majority Text," abbreviated MT. These are sometimes spoken of as being the same thing. The Majority Text, however, is exactly what its name implies. It is compiled by taking the simple majority of manuscript evidence to decide which variations to use in the Greek text. While the Textus Receptus is based on a particular small set of manuscripts, the Majority Text is based on giving every manuscript a vote, as it were, and so they do not match each other. While this approach may appeal to democratic sensibilities, it is skewed toward more recent texts and away from more ancient ones, simply because more recent texts survive. Further, the text assembled by majority vote does not actually match any manuscript which we possess. This means it represents a hypothetical text rather than a real one.

Following Stephanus's publication, translation efforts followed his methodology by integrating other manuscripts into his text. The translators of the King James Version did this, integrating their available manuscripts with the then current published edition of the Greek New Testament. Over the next two centuries, the number of manuscripts available continued to steadily increase, and new finds were integrated into the published text piecemeal along the way. Historically, at no stage was the printed Greek text declared to be inspired, perfect, or finished.

In the nineteenth century, these finds reached a sort of critical mass. Two men, Brooke Foss Westcott and Fenton John Anthony Hort, set out to catalog and account for all the then known New Testament manuscripts. Westcott and Hort first developed the concept of text types described in the previous chapter. They also established the Alexandrian text type as the "neutral text" and utilized it, as the oldest form of the text in their estimation, as the primary text for their Greek New Testament published in 1881. While many other manuscripts had been incorporated into the Greek New Testament text over time, its base until their day had been the Byzantine manuscripts of the Textus Receptus. While all the textual information, and more which the pair had developed themselves, was still included in their printed text, the text now had a different base.

Since the publication of Westcott and Hort's New Testament, the same methodology has been followed in printing the critical edition of the Greek text as was previously followed with the Textus Receptus. New manuscript finds are incorporated into the notes on the text until such time as a great weight of evidence has been produced for a preferred reading, at which point the base text is changed and the former text is moved to the notes. While the Greek New Testament has gone through several dozen editions since 1881, each edition is a developmental stage from Westcott and Hort's New Testament. All the major fresh English translations of the New Testament produced since the end of the nineteenth century have been based on this critical text, though there are also more recent revisions of English translations originally based on some stage of the Textus Receptus.

Methods of Translation

IN ADDITION TO WORKING FROM different base texts, English translations of the Bible also follow various strategies or theories of translation. While there are a handful of biblical translations produced by a single person, the most well-known, popular, and commonly encountered English versions of the Scriptures were translated by committees. Especially in recent times, these committees have grown increasingly diverse. This is most often a good thing, as a diverse translation committee helps to prevent sectarian bias from intruding. In addition, this diversity has, in several more recent translations, led to the presence, and therefore the influence, of Orthodox Christians in these committees.

A variety of motives have moved the formation of these committees to produce new translations of the Scriptures and to update existing ones. Some of these motives, such as concern over the sectarian nature of existing translations or the desire to take into account new textual discoveries, are laudatory. Others are more mercenary. The current proliferation of English versions in the United States, for example, is motivated largely by the desire of each major publishing company to be able to license its own version of the Scriptures. To paraphrase St. Paul, however, whether for good motives or for ill, the Scriptures continue to be translated.

When reading the Scriptures in English, it is important to understand the translation strategy of the text that is being read.

It is also important, as often as possible, to read the Scriptures in more than one translation. Reading from only one English translation is akin to hearing only one preacher or learning from one teacher: the preacher or teacher may pass on biases, blind spots, misinterpretations, or errors directly to the hearer. Just as a student reads more than one book in researching a topic, so also in reading and studying the Scriptures, it is wise to read more than one translation.

What separates the various translation strategies used to produce English Bible versions is the degree to which they stress accuracy to their base texts over against readability. Those that are based on making a word-for-word translation, sometimes even to the point of being grammatically incorrect in English, use a strategy called "formal equivalence." Other translations focus more on readability and have as their goal the communication of a concept conveyed by the original language to a concept in the English language. These translations use a strategy referred to as "dynamic equivalence."

Formal equivalence translations have the benefit of bringing the reader very close to the wording of the original language. They have the drawback of sometimes failing to render as understandable to English readers the ideas contained. Both Hebrew and Greek grammar are quite different from English grammar. Dynamic equivalence translations have the benefit of being more readable and conveying more of the sense of the text, but they are another step removed from the original language and therefore engage in a greater degree of interpretation. This requires an awareness of the filters through which the Scriptures are passing before reaching the reader.

The other major category of Bibles in the English language is not really the product of a translation strategy per se. These Bibles, generally referred to as "paraphrases," attempt to convey the general ideas of the Bible in modern, sometimes even colloquial, English. In many cases, these paraphrases are based not on a new translation of the original texts, but on another English version that they rephrase. Examples of paraphrases are Bibles such as The Living Bible or The Message. This type of Bible is not suitable for the study of the Scriptures by Orthodox Christians. In many cases, in attempting to simplify, they distort important theological points concerning, for example, the Holy Trinity and the Person of Jesus Christ. To read one of these texts is not to read the Scriptures, but to read someone's interpretation of the Scriptures.

In addition to the name of the version or translation, there are other labels that commonly appear on English Bibles. Study Bibles contain notes written by a person or committee, usually in the form of extensive footnotes beneath the text. Other than those in the *Orthodox Study Bible*, none of these notes are written from an Orthodox Christian perspective, despite the vast array of study Bibles. Typically, the study Bibles produced by evangelical Protestant publishing houses in the United States contain notes that will express a variety of interpretations of a given passage, reflecting the many Protestant interpretations of that text. Typically, the notes ignore the Orthodox reading of the texts in question—even the views of the Church Fathers.

These study Bibles, however, must be distinguished from reference Bibles and other Bibles that contain extensive textual notes. Reference Bibles contain notes, often in the margins, that show the connections between various Scriptures, such as New

Testament references to the Old Testament. These can be very helpful for biblical study. Other Bibles that can be very helpful include extensive textual notation, usually in the form of footnotes, that describe the variations in Hebrew, Greek, and other languages from the text used in the translation. When reading the Bible in translation, these notes can be the best source for understanding both the original text and the sorts of decisions that have been made by the translators.

Major English Translations

ANY SURVEY OF ENGLISH TRANSLATIONS of the Bible must begin with the King James Version. The King James Bible is not only the most popular English Bible in history, and still in print in a wide variety of editions today, but it is a literary masterpiece in its own right. King James of England commissioned his translation at the beginning of the seventeenth century to replace the increasingly popular Geneva Bible. The Geneva Bible was perceived to be decidedly Calvinist in character and, more importantly to James, anti-monarchic. He therefore convened a committee of top scholars to create a new translation that would be called the Authorized Version. The text was translated from a version of the Textus Receptus tradition, though the actual base text of the King James Version does not precisely match any version of the Textus Receptus that had been published. The committee used not only the then current edition of the Textus Receptus but also the best additional manuscripts that they were able to acquire. The first edition of the King James Version was printed in 1611. Printings of this original version are still available.

The vast majority of KJV Bibles available for purchase are not the 1611 edition, however. Immediately after its original publication, revisions began. In fact, the King James Version was revised more than a dozen times, with thousands of changes made over the course of the following century and a half. Most of these changes took the form of corrections. Others involved standardizing and updating weights and measures. The KJV as we know it today is actually the Oxford standard edition produced in 1769. After this edition, the normal revision process ceased, but not because the KJV was considered perfect. Rather, while its literary nature and quality for its time of origin were still impressive, textual finds and advances in the understanding of ancient Greek and Hebrew began to necessitate not a further revision, but a new translation.

In the wake of many other more modern translations, Thomas Nelson Publishing produced the New King James Version (NKJV) in 1982. The selling point of this translation was that it used the same texts as the King James Version, but it was translated into more readable, modern English. Because the original was based on a relatively small number of manuscripts, which were also the best available to translators at the time, certain peculiarities of those texts entered into the English translation, including additional verses where interpretations entered the text, and even a few textual errors. These were discovered and removed from other modern English translations, to the consternation of those who had grown used to the readings of the KJV. Such was the backlash that an entire King James–only movement was spawned within American Protestantism, bolstered by sometimes elaborate conspiracy theories.

The New King James Version promised to deliver to this audience a more readable version of the Scriptures that included all the original KJV's peculiarities. While specific "problem passages" were indeed maintained, the NKJV was, in fact, a new translation from more modern base texts. The Old Testament was translated from the then current critical edition of the Hebrew text, while the New Testament was translated from the then current edition of the Textus Receptus, an edition published in 1881. Significant portions of that Greek text reflected no manuscript but were translated back into Greek from the King James Version. In the end, the NKJV converted few of those devoted to the original KJV. It is a readable text but reflects neither the actual base text of the King James Version nor the better manuscript evidence which had been discovered since. It is a dynamic equivalence translation that lacks much of the literary quality of its predecessor. The NKJV translators also did not translate the books of the Old Testament beyond the Jewish canon, unlike the translators of the KJV. The New Testament text of the *Orthodox Study Bible* is based on the NKJV, and the Old Testament text is highly influenced by it.

The English Bible tradition that has enjoyed the most long-term success other than the King James tradition is the Revised Standard Version (RSV). The RSV was first published in 1952 and was a product of a translation committee formed by the National Council of Churches, with the work later taken over by Oxford University. This text is notable in that it was the first English version of the Bible whose translation received input from Orthodox Christian representatives. Once Oxford took over the work, it expanded the Old Testament translation to include the entirety of the Greek and Slavonic canons in 1977.

Many of the features taken for granted in modern Bibles, such as the substitution of "LORD" for the name "Yahweh" rather than "Jehovah" in the Old Testament, began in the RSV. The Oxford Annotated Bible is one common form of the RSV text with the full Old Testament included. The text straddles several lines: It is at once a new translation and a revision of the KJV, as the latter text was taken heavily into account in the production of the RSV translation. It also seeks to make accuracy and readability equal priorities, taking an approach between formal and dynamic equivalence.

The RSV itself has had two major published revisions. The first is the New Revised Standard Version (NRSV), published in 1989. It is translated from the same textual base as the RSV but represents an attempt to further modernize the language. One of the main changes, for example, was the use of gender-inclusive language outside of references to God. This version also made clear paragraph breaks and inserted its own interpretive paragraph headings. The breaks in the text do not match any lectionary, and it represents no significant improvement over the original RSV.

More successful has been the English Standard Version (ESV), which was produced in the 1990s by a committee of scholars dissatisfied with the popularity of dynamic equivalence translations that dominated the marketplace at that time. The ESV is not really a new translation, however, but a revision of the original RSV text. Ninety-four percent of the English Standard Version text is identical to that of the RSV. The 6 percent difference is not primarily retranslation but amendment of the base text. The scholars had access to the Dead Sea Scrolls information with regard to the Old Testament and many new manuscripts and, in particular, early papyrus finds regarding the New Testament. The difference between the two translations reflects these updates. The ESV committee did produce an updated translation of the larger Christian Old Testament canon, though at the time of this writing it has only recently become widely available. Most printed editions of the ESV in the United States include only the Rabbinic canon of the Old Testament.

Since its publication in 2001, the English Standard Version has become very popular and with good reason. It represents the most accurate and readable English rendition of the Hebrew Old Testament and Greek New Testament to date. It is highly recommended for regular day-to-day reading.

The most popular Bible in the period before the publication of the ESV and the main source of its translators' dissatisfaction was the New International Version (NIV). The NIV began as a product of a Dutch Reformed denomination in the United States but invited the participation of the broader evangelical Protestant world. It is a dynamic equivalence translation that focuses on readability. The language is decidedly less formal than similar translations, using a large number of contractions, for example, in the text. It is also prone to euphemisms, particularly in the Old Testament, where the literal meaning of the text might be considered inappropriate or unseemly. Nevertheless, from its publication in 1978, it became extremely popular, particularly in study Bible form, among evangelical Protestant communities. There is an unsubtle Protestant and, in places, even Calvinist slant to the translation. No translation was made of the broader Christian Old Testament canon.

More recently, a major revision of the NIV was produced in 2005 and called Today's New International Version (TNIV). Though this Bible has since been discontinued in favor of a new, updated version of the NIV that incorporates many of its changes, copies are still somewhat widely available. The two major changes instituted in the TNIV were the further use of modernized colloquial English and the introduction of gender-inclusive language when not referring to God. These changes served only to move the translation in English even further from the original text while continuing the overall biases of the original NIV.

The New American Standard Bible (NASB) is the English Bible that moves furthest in the direction of formal equivalence, often accomplished at the expense of readability. The primary effort of the translators was to convey the original text word for word, as well as mirror the grammar and syntax of the original languages. This often does not conform to a good English style. The NASB is therefore helpful as a second translation to be used for study alongside a more readable text. Its literalness allows freer renderings in other translations to be tested against the original, at least to a certain extent, even for English-only readers. Since its publication in 1971, the NASB has been updated several times, most recently in 1995. These updates are not efforts to amend the English text, but rather to take into account more recent manuscript finds and textual scholarship.

Finally, the best English Bible for those interested in a more serious and detailed study is the New English Translation (NET). The NET was produced by the Biblical Studies Foundation and published by Biblical Studies Press. In its full-notes edition, it contains the most copious textual notes of any

English Bible, giving the reader unparalleled access to the original manuscripts. The text was released in 2006 in both print and digital formats. The digital format of the NET is available free of charge, while printed editions are rendered affordable by allowing access to the translation's copyright.

There are literally dozens of other versions and translations of the Scriptures in English, far more than could be discussed in detail in this book. I highlighted the translations discussed above because they are the most common and readily available in the United States at the time of this writing. Also included are the versions that deserve the most attention from Orthodox Christians interested in the serious reading and study of the Scriptures in English. We could have a similar discussion in equal detail of the translation tradition of the Scriptures in many other languages.

The versions that have been discussed above in a positive sense should be taken to constitute recommendations. However, a significant number of Bibles should be avoided: paraphrases such as The Message, The Living Bible, or Today's English Version skew the biblical text in a way that is unhelpful. The New World Translation is not a translation but an edit of the King James Version to make it conform to the teachings of the Watchtower Bible and Tract Society, also known as Jehovah's Witnesses. In the other versions discussed above, even those such as the less-than-ideal New International Version, there is enough of the Scriptures for an Orthodox Christian to hear their voice. Better versions will bring one into even closer contact with the text of the Scriptures and, more importantly, the Person of Jesus Christ whom they reveal.

CHAPTER FIVE

How Should I Read My Bible?

M ODERN CHRISTIANS GENERALLY SHARE THE
impression that they ought to spend more time reading
the Bible. While justifications for why we have failed to do so
will vary, the truth is often that we simply don't know how. Even
with only the shorter Protestant set of books, an English Bible is
thick, with fairly small print. Often the first question is "Where
should I begin?"

We are extremely familiar with certain sections of the text,
mostly in the New Testament and mostly in the Gospels. We are
not even aware of the existence of certain books in the Old Testament, and maybe even in the New Testament Epistles. Some
books tell straightforward "Bible stories," while others, like the
Book of Revelation, offer bizarre phantasmagorias of monsters
and plagues. In between, a lot of the Bible just seems kind of
boring and irrelevant.

Many people make repeated attempts to read the Bible in the
way that we typically read books. They begin on the first page
of the Book of Genesis and try to read straight through. Except
for a few genealogies in Genesis, most of that first book and the

first half of Exodus consist of narrative stories that maintain the average person's interest fairly well. By the second half of Exodus, however, one is greeted by lengthy descriptions of the measurements and raw materials to construct various items of furniture in the tabernacle. Powering through the rest of Exodus, the reader then finds Leviticus, which consists almost entirely of detailed commandments on mildew removal and the correct separation of the entrails of sacrificial animals. Somewhere in Leviticus or Numbers, these attempts to read the Bible tend to fizzle out.

More important than mustering the enthusiasm to scan every page of the text visually, however, is understanding what is being read. For the reading of the Holy Scriptures to bear any fruit, we must take in and comprehend them. Merely "muscling through" texts like Leviticus, Numbers, or the lengthy genealogies of 1 and 2 Chronicles is a pointless exercise if the words are just meaningless or represent cryptic riddles on the printed page. The Ethiopian eunuch summed up the problem in the earliest days of Christianity: "How can I understand if there is no one who teaches me?" (Acts 8:31).

There are three major aspects of reading and understanding the Scriptures. Each of these three benefits from study and effort, but none of them requires advanced degrees or knowledge of ancient languages. Anyone with access to the Scriptures can begin to read them with understanding right now.

Reading: What Does the Text Say?

DETERMINING WHAT THE TEXT SAYS seems kind of obvious. You just read the text on the page. As has already been discussed, understanding what the text actually says is not just a matter of assuming that one particular English translation, even a good one, has brought the meaning of the original text in the original languages into our language perfectly. In every translation effort, decisions are made. To truly read and learn from the Scriptures, we cannot simply assume that all these decisions were necessarily the right ones.

At the same time, at least in our contemporary age of access to countless translations and voluminous information about the text of the Scriptures through electronic and other means, no one needs to go down the rabbit hole of mastering ancient languages simply to understand the Bible. Language study is not even necessary for the average layperson to read the Bible seriously. In fact, a little language knowledge can be a dangerous thing. Truly mastering biblical Hebrew or Greek takes years of intensive, directed study. Without a knack for it, this process can be difficult and tedious. Many people choose to dabble in the biblical languages in order to help them understand the Scriptures. While their intent is good, they often over-interpret and over-apply the bits and pieces of Hebrew or Greek that they learn, yielding false insights. It is much better to read an English translation and live with an imperfect or less-than-detailed understanding of the text than to become confident in bad interpretations.

How does someone thread this needle between over-confidence in a single translation and being unable to understand it without advanced language knowledge? A good first step is to compare translations. This no longer has to involve the juggling of multiple physical Bibles, as the reader can find dozens of translations available online and search them simultaneously. If an English reader knows which translations are more literal and accurate and which are more interpretive, he or she can get a broad idea of the underlying text through the variations in translation. For devotional reading, it is fine to choose one translation that is comfortable and stick with it. When questions arise, comparing multiple translations is the easiest place to begin.

Most solid Bible translations also include footnotes. Study Bible notes will vary in quality and character based on those notes' authorship and the intended audience. On the other hand, basic footnotes are merely short notes related to the translation to try to make the original more accessible in English. One very common type of footnote will begin with the abbreviation "*lit.*" This is an abbreviation for "literally." Sometimes words or phrasing will carry meaning in one language that they don't carry in another. For example, in British English, the phrase "let's get a shift on" means "let's hurry." In translating a text containing that phrase for an American or non-English audience, the translator might choose to translate it as "let's hurry." Then, to give better access to the original, the translator might place a footnote saying, "*lit.* get a shift on."

Another common footnote will talk about other versions of the text beyond the one that is the basis for the translation. Sometimes a word or phrase is found in some manuscripts and not others. Sometimes one word will appear in some manuscripts, and a similar but different word will appear in others. In most cases, the translator will decide which version is the best and most reliable and translate it into the text's main body, then place a footnote explaining that some manuscripts read differently. Similarly, if other ancient translations of the text, such as the Greek Old Testament tradition, the Aramaic, or the Syriac, have a different or interesting translation for a certain text, it will appear in a footnote.

Interpreting: What Does the Text Mean?

ONCE WHAT A TEXT SAYS is clear, the next step is to determine what it means. This is the task of interpretation. Words are symbols that refer to something beyond themselves. A word invokes a concept or the memory of an object, person, or activity. Placing words in a meaningful order on the page relates these concepts to each other and produces a combined effect. If the words have not been clearly nailed down, determining what they are intended to communicate is impossible. The meaning will always remain as ambiguous as the wording of the text is. Determining meaning is all about context. Since no one sits down and reads through the entire Bible in one sitting, a person is always reading portions of the text.

SCRIPTURAL CONTEXT

THE FIRST LEVEL OF CONTEXT involved in interpreting the Bible is the context of the particular portion of the Scriptures being read. In the case of Psalms and Proverbs, this is sometimes difficult, because portions of the text have little relationship to the parts immediately before and after. An individual psalm or set of proverbs might have been written centuries before or after the material that precedes and follows it. These books represent disparate elements that have been collected together. Most of the Scriptures, however, are either a continuous narrative or a continuous argument. This means that a particular story or section of an epistle is related to the story or section that it follows. The part that follows it will likewise continue to build from the portion being read.

The context of the surrounding text is an important check on possible interpretations. Nearly any text or portion of the text can be taken or argued to mean nearly anything when isolated and out of context. However, we quickly narrow this wide range of possibilities if we consider only those interpretations that make sense following the preceding text. Likewise, if the next text would make no sense following a certain interpretation, that interpretation can be ruled out. The meaning of any given piece of Scripture must make sense as a link in a chain of meaning for any given book of the Bible. The authors of Scripture do not abruptly talk about completely unrelated matters in the middle of a discussion without clearly indicating that they are changing topics.

Often, because of the way in which we read Scripture, we miss this most basic level of context. If, for example, we follow the Church's daily Scripture readings, we will read small sections each day. Becoming familiar with the individual units of Scripture in this way is important, and the liturgical arrangement of texts conveys its own level of meaning. As a supplement to this, it is also helpful to read an entire book in one sitting. The average person can read even relatively long biblical books like the Gospels or one of the historical books of the Old Testament in one afternoon. Having an idea of the whole story, as it were, can help a great deal in the understanding of each part when we later read them separately.

HISTORICAL CONTEXT

THE NEXT LEVEL OF CONTEXT is historical. The Scriptures were composed and compiled over the course of many centuries. The time period that the text describes will affect its meaning. The Old Testament covers a vast span of time. Is a story from before the time of Moses and the beginning of Israel? After? Is it before or after the beginning of Israel's monarchy? Does it take place during the period in which Israel and Judah were separate nations, and if so, in which one? Is it a story from the Babylonian exile? The New Testament covers a smaller span of time but represents a very different situation from any of the Old Testament contexts. Understanding where in biblical history a reading is located will also rule out interpretive possibilities. To inject certain ideas or premises forward or backward in history will produce anachronisms and confuse the meaning of the text.

The historical situation of any given text also opens up the possibility of learning about a broader context. What was the culture of the author like? What were the surrounding cultures like? What other texts, outside the Bible, might a given author have been reading and interacting with? These questions can become rabbit holes, but taking advantage of this historical knowledge doesn't require spending years studying ancient history. For example, most study Bibles will include basic historical details about cities, people, and places that will help create this broader sense of context.

Some texts of Scripture have two contexts: a context of the events being described and a context at the time of writing. The Book of Genesis, for example, was clearly written long after the events described there. Abraham lived at one time in the world's history in a particular culture and interacted with other cultures of that time. Moses and the later editors of the Torah lived centuries later and came from different cultures. When Christ spoke, He spoke to actual living humans whom He encountered, and He addressed them directly. Those words were recorded some decades later by His apostles, who saw an importance to Christ's words beyond just the person or group of people to whom He originally spoke. The reality of these two contexts doesn't confuse meaning. In fact, it helps develop the meaning of the text. First, the story's initial context should be described, as well as what the words and actions meant in that context. Second, we can investigate their context within the later written work and their ongoing significance. The apostles made deliberate choices in what they recorded and what they chose not to record. As St. John pointed out, if everything Christ said and did were written, the world would not be large enough to contain all the books (John 21:25).

CANONICAL CONTEXT

THE SCRIPTURES AS A WHOLE represent a context as well. This context is sometimes called the canonical context. The various texts that make up the Scriptures have been edited, gathered, and collected into a library that exercises authority in the community of the Church. The Church brought them together and understood them as relating to one another. Over the Bible's history, its books have been placed in various orders, and so the order in and of itself should not be a basis for interpretation.

The texts that make up the Bible interact with one another in various ways. The most obvious may be the latter portions of the Old Testament and the New Testament that quote earlier parts of the Old Testament. These quotations function somewhat differently than modern citations. Because the Scriptures did not have chapter and verse references until the medieval period, a few numbers were not sufficient to indicate a particular passage. Because they were hand copied and existed for many centuries on scrolls, page numbers were likewise not a possibility. To refer to a passage of the Scriptures, then, the author would quote the first line of a section of text to refer to the whole passage. In the same way, someone today quoting the first lyrics of a song might bring the entire song to mind. Ancient people primarily heard the Scriptures read and chanted, rather than reading them for themselves.

When the Scriptures interpret other portions of the Scriptures, everyone can be assured that they are being handled correctly. Sometimes, the meaning of a quotation in the New Testament or how it relates to the point being made is unclear. The first interpretive task is to go back to the source of the quotation and read the entire passage. With an understanding of the text being quoted, the later text will often become much clearer. Interpretations that require the New Testament author to be interpreting the Old Testament poorly should be ruled out. This same procedure is important when the New Testament mentions biblical figures. When the New Testament authors refer to Abraham or Noah or Jacob, they are referring to the actual person. Because they knew the text of the Old Testament very well, they wouldn't use biblical examples or make points that wouldn't make sense to others who knew the Scriptures just as well. Making an argument that they couldn't support would have done the opposite of helping them make their point about Christ and the gospel.

In addition to outright quotations of the Old Testament, we find countless allusions and other, subtler references to the earlier Scriptures in the New Testament. English translations often obscure these connections and repetitions of words and phrases and require more attention to discern. Most English Bibles have Old Testaments translated from the Hebrew and New Testaments translated from the Greek. Even competent and attentive translators may not translate an Old Testament text identically to a related New Testament text that is alluding to it. A great aid to discovering these connections is the references found in most English Bibles, often in a center column between the two columns of text. Any given verse in a reference Bible will have a short list of other related scriptures. Following these trails to other texts will often illuminate all the texts involved.

Applying: How Is the Text Relevant to Me and My Life?

ONCE WE UNDERSTAND WHAT A text says and what it means, a remaining step is to read the Bible in a profitable way. The text's details and even its meaning can all be considered in the abstract, as an intellectual exercise. Verses can become proof texts—isolated statements to use in theological arguments that ultimately just devolve into word games. These arguments may be entertaining or the preferred mode of distraction for certain people, but they do nothing to help anyone live the Christian life. The Bible is not a "how-to" manual with techniques to become more like Christ or achieve salvation. At the same time, if we do not apply what we read there, then we become like those who hear the word but do not do what it says (James 1:23–24). The time we spend reading and seeking to understand the Scriptures ends up being wasted because it bears no fruit.

This final step, the application of the text, can be the most difficult step in the interpretive process. While perhaps interesting at some level, some texts do not seem to have much relevance to the day-to-day struggles of a twenty-first-century Christian. It is hard to see how the genealogical descent of an ancient nation that has long since collapsed relates to repentance from sin. It is difficult to see how a story that may be violent or just outright strange to contemporary eyes is going to help me draw closer to Christ. It is not obvious that reading about a pagan prophet's argument with a talking donkey will assist my prayer life in any way.

At the level of interpretation, a given text could mean a wide variety of things. Many of those options, however, can be pruned away by paying close attention to context. But the application of a given text allows for an even wider range of variation. When we read of a biblical personage performing a particular action, should we understand that we are to do as that person did? Or is that person being held up as a bad example? The New Testament tells us repeatedly that the Old Testament speaks concerning Christ. The New Testament authors will often connect Old Testament figures and their actions and experiences to Christ through analogy, allegory, typology, or the idea of prophetic fulfillment. When I read a story and try to do that, when do I see something that is really there in the text, and when am I stretching? Even once I make a connection to Christ, that still fails to answer the question about what I should do with it in my actual lived experience.

CHURCH TRADITION AND THE FATHERS

AS CONTEXT HELPED RESTRAIN AND guide our understanding of texts' meaning, tradition moderates and directs our application of the Scriptures. Christianity existed for nearly two thousand years before this author and any readers of this book were born. For century after century, Christians have sought to follow Christ in their lives and come to know Him more deeply. They have done this in a wide variety of cultures, places, and times in all kinds of material situations. They have not only sought to do this, but they have succeeded. Generations of saints have lived as Christians, found salvation, and become like Christ in their lives. Part of this process for them was hearing the Scriptures and putting them into practice. Their sanctity is testimony to the fact that they did so in appropriate and correct ways.

The way the Scriptures have been interpreted and applied through the history of the Church under the Holy Spirit's guidance is available in multiple areas of our received tradition. One important repository is the writings of the Fathers. The Fathers are not only those commonly called Church Fathers, chiefly hierarchs of the Church's early centuries of life. The Fathers also include later saints and Christian writers and, possibly most importantly, monastic fathers and mothers who read and interpret the Scriptures based on their own experience of Christ and of salvation.

A number of potential pitfalls exist in utilizing the writings of the Fathers to interpret the Scriptures. There may be a temptation to skim through or search for patristic citations that support the interpretation or point of view that we already want to hold. Additionally, we sometimes forget that the Fathers wrote not in English but in other languages, primarily ancient languages. Everything written in this book about translating and interpreting the Scriptures is equally true of translating and interpreting the Fathers.

The majority of the writings of the Fathers have not been translated into English, and so it is very dangerous to generalize based on the portions of their writings that we have available. Further, the vast majority of the translations that we do have were not made by Orthodox Christians. In the same way that one's own theology may color the way one translates the Scriptures, it may color the way in which one translates and reads the Fathers and other early Christian writers. Just as happens with Scripture, Orthodox, Roman Catholic, and Protestant apologists can produce quotes from the Fathers that seem to support their positions.

As contemporary Western people, we have been trained to think about interpretation in a modern, scientific way. We tend to think that every verse in the Scriptures has one particular meaning, and that the goal of interpretation is to find that meaning. We then construct methodologies to do so. Further, we assume that the Fathers saw the Scriptures in the same way, and that a careful reading of a given Father will allow one to discern and reproduce that methodology. Modern people then categorize these methodologies so that one group of Fathers, sometimes associated with Antioch, is labeled as reading the text "literally" while another, sometimes associated with Alexandria, is labeled as reading it "allegorically." A sustained reading of the Fathers reveals that these generalizations are simply false.

This division between literal and allegorical approaches in the Fathers is an attempt to take the modern debate, described in chapter 1 of this book, between "fundamentalists" and "liberals" and project it into ancient Church history. Identifying certain Fathers as allegorists is seen to provide license for more liberal parties to take freedoms with the text of Scripture, often far beyond what any of the Fathers in question would accept. Identifying certain other Fathers, or sometimes even "the Fathers" as a whole, as being literalists is used to demand compliance with an equally modern, quasi-scientific reading of the Scriptures that the Fathers in question wouldn't recognize.

The error here is found in the reality that the Fathers understood multiple levels of meaning within the text of the Scriptures. The Fathers all accept the reality and truth of the literal meaning of the Scriptures. For them, the literal meaning is the meaning that the text has in its context, whether that be as an event within an overarching historical narrative, a line within a piece of poetry, or a particular point being made within an epistle. In addition, the Fathers acknowledge another level of meaning that connects any portion of the Scriptures to Christ, the Word of God, and, through Christ, to Christians living in any and every era of the Church's life.

A given Father will often place more emphasis in any given writing on one or the other level of meaning. If engaged in theological debate with someone denying the truth or reality of the literal level of the text, a Father will often focus on that aspect of meaning. When teaching and guiding their Christian contemporaries, they will often focus on how the text leads the hearers and readers to Christ and brings Him into their daily lives. The truth is that these two levels of meaning require each other. If the Scriptures are not true in their original, contextual sense, then no other application can be certain. If the Scriptures are true only in their original, contextual sense, then they are irrelevant to anyone living after the first century AD except as a historical curiosity.

Rather than proof-texting or generalizing, seeing the ways in which people advanced in the life in Christ guides how we might do the same thing in our own lives. If my understanding of how a portion of Scripture should be applied is found nowhere among the saints and holy Fathers who came before us, then I am wrong. At the same time, if I find a Church Father, or even several, who agree with me, and I quote them to justify my beliefs and actions, it's no guarantee that I am on the right track. In between these two is the realm of continuity. We are called not merely to parrot the sayings of the Fathers about Scripture, but to read and apply Scripture in the ways they did. Each of us should seek to live a life in Christ that is in continuity with the lives lived by those who came before us—although they will not be identical due to differences in time, place, and culture.

THE LITURGICAL SERVICES OF THE CHURCH

ANOTHER IMPORTANT SOURCE FOR THE interpretation and application of the Scriptures is the liturgical services of the Church. Various texts of Scripture are read at certain times, related to certain feasts, or sung along with other passages to which they are connected. The Old Testament texts read at Great Vespers before feasts relate to those feasts in the same way that a feast's epistle and Gospel readings do. Some Scripture passages are connected to liturgical actions, such as Psalm 24/23 being quoted during the knocking on the church doors at Pascha in some traditions. These liturgical texts are not the creative expression of an individual who lived at a recent point in history. Rather, these words and practices that form worship have been handed down to us to preserve a particularly important way of reading and interpreting Scripture. The liturgical use of the Scriptures allows us to learn and internalize them in a different way than does rote memorization or academic study.

A Christian does not come to read the Scriptures alone and isolated, left to his or her own devices to try to come to the right conclusions that will allow him or her to do what is needed to find salvation. A Christian comes to the Scriptures with the aid and enlightenment of the Holy Spirit. But merely asserting the presence of the Holy Spirit is still a nebulous thing. Anyone can make any interpretation and claim to have been guided by the Spirit. Multiple readers can come to contradictory interpretations, yet all make that same claim. The Holy Spirit, however, not only indwells and guides individual human persons. He also lives in and guides the Church as a whole through the centuries of her shared life. As St. Paul says, the Spirit is not a Spirit of division, but of good order (1 Cor. 14:33). The Church is our best, and, in truth, an infallible guide to following the way through this world that leads to salvation in Christ, including the reading, understanding, and application of the Holy Scriptures.

Conclusion

T HE BIBLE, THE CHRISTIAN SCRIPTURES, occupies a central place in the life of the Orthodox Church and her worship. Scripture is read in every service, often in large quantity; where Scripture is not being directly quoted in the liturgy, it is being referenced or is the subject of allusion. This is one way in which the Orthodox Church teaches her members that the Scriptures should be at the center of their lives as well. The Scriptures both convey to us the Person of Jesus Christ and give us the language that allows our hearts and souls to respond to Him. In Orthodox worship and prayer, we hear the Scriptures and respond with the words of the Scriptures. The Bible is what we inhale and exhale to breathe and spiritually live.

For this sort of Christian life to be possible, Orthodox Christians must give the Scriptures this place in our lives. The Church gives us the lectionary and reading schedules, and the divisions of the Psalms, just as she gives us written prayers to allow us to make a beginning. But this is the beginning of our participation in the Bible, not the end, just as it is the beginning of our life of prayer. The more deeply we immerse ourselves in the Scriptures, the more we become able to breathe them. As the Bible itself tells us, it is not enough for the Scriptures to be written in scrolls and books. They must also be written upon our hearts (Josh. 1:8, Jer. 31:33, Rom. 2:15, Heb. 8:10).

The ultimate author of the Scriptures is also the Author of the universe. The words of Scripture point ultimately to the Word of God, our Lord Jesus Christ. Through the Scriptures, Christ reveals Himself to us, and we come to know Him. The Scriptures are not a place to do research about Christ or to study historical beliefs about the Messiah and Jesus' fulfillment of that role. Through the Scriptures we encounter the risen, living Christ directly, just as those saints, prophets, and apostles about whom we read encountered Him in ages past. Through Christ, we see who God, the Holy Trinity, is. We come to understand the character of God and how He has acted in His creation throughout its history. This attunes our spiritual senses to be able to encounter Him anew in all our life in creation today.

This book is intended to provide an entry point into the world of the Scriptures. By understanding what the Scriptures are, whence they came, how they developed, and how to begin to read them, the Scriptures become less opaque, less foreign, and less daunting. While we may often struggle with what certain passages say to us about our own sin and need of repentance, there is no reason to struggle with the Scriptures themselves. They were written concerning the experiences of people like us, by people like us, for people like us. They have been preserved through the centuries by people like us. All of this has taken place through the guidance and working of the Holy Spirit. So, if we too acquire the Holy Spirit, we will discover that the Scriptures are truly ours.

Further Reading

THERE IS NOT A GREAT body of literature concerning biblical studies from an Orthodox Christian perspective. The present volume represents an attempt to begin to fill this gap. For this reason, most of the books listed below for further reading are not written by Orthodox authors or scholars. Where it is known and relevant to understanding a given text, the point of view of the author will be noted. Obviously, there is a great deal more to be said about all aspects of the Bible and the texts that comprise it than could even be mentioned in this book. This annotated bibliography will focus on making a few recommendations regarding each of the topics that have been addressed.

An excellent source for delving deeper into several of the subjects discussed in this book is Paul D. Wegner's *The Journey from Texts to Translations* (Baker Academic, 1999). This one volume, though academic in nature, discusses writing and literacy in the ancient world, forms of biblical manuscripts, textual criticism, translation methodology, and the English Bible tradition to the end of the twentieth century. While Wegner is not Orthodox, this text focuses on supplying the reader with a wealth of factual information and data from which we can draw our own conclusions within the context of our tradition.

The most important introductory text to the field of New Testament textual criticism is *The Text of the New Testament: Its Transmission, Corruption, and Restoration* by Bruce Metzger (Oxford, 2005). It is currently in a fourth edition and has been updated by Bart Ehrman, Metzger's most prominent student, since Metzger's death. Metzger was a committed Protestant. Bart Ehrman is a prominent non-Christian scholar of the Bible. Anyone who is considering entering the field of textual criticism, and certainly anyone doing academic work in the field, begins with this text.

The purpose of Metzger's book is to orient the reader in the materials and methods of textual criticism as the discipline currently exists academically. Where it describes a perspective or a conclusion, it is the perspective or conclusion of the current scholarly consensus. This consensus is not always in line with the Orthodox understanding of Scripture. This is still, however, a very valuable work for several reasons. It describes the current consensus regardless of whether an Orthodox scholar would agree with it. It also describes the methodology that has been used to arrive at those conclusions, allowing the reader to understand the various arguments involved. Finally, and most importantly, it supplies an immense amount of factual data regarding the manuscripts of the New Testament, which is what anyone proposing an understanding of the New Testament text must take into account.

In the English Bible tradition, the King James Version looms large. Several good books have been written on the translation of the KJV, which is a masterpiece of literature outside of the

role it has played in Western religious culture, including Orthodox churches in the United States. Gustavus S. Paine's *The Men
behind the King James Version* (Baker, 1977) is an older book
about the King James translators but is rightly considered a classic. Alister McGrath's *In the Beginning* (Anchor, 2002) is a more
recent historical account of the origins of the King James Bible.
McGrath focuses on the British cultural currents that factored
into the creation of the KJV and its cultural impact. The most
detailed historical account of the proceedings has been published by Adam Nicolson, *God's Secretaries: The Making of the
King James Bible* (Harper, 2003).

Michael Kruger, a Presbyterian scholar, has done significant
work on the topic of the canon. As a Protestant commenting
on the Old Testament canon, he differs on several points with
the Orthodox understanding of Scripture. However, most of
Kruger's work has focused on the New Testament, and he is a
rare scholar who is completely honest to his data even when it
doesn't perfectly conform to his own religious mindset. His two
books on the New Testament canon, *Canon Revisited* (Cross-
way, 2012) and *The Question of Canon* (IVP Academic, 2013),
give a good historical overview of the actual community pro-
cesses through which the New Testament texts came to hold
their canonical authority.

A renewed interest in the Greek Old Testament tradition outside of Greek-speaking Orthodoxy has produced some excellent
resources on its history and on textual criticism of that Old Testament tradition. Karen H. Jobes and Moisés Silva's *Invitation
to the Septuagint* (Baker, 2005) is not extremely readable. It is,
however, a solid reference work for issues regarding the various
strands of the Greek Old Testament tradition and text-critical

issues. A much more reader-friendly introductory text to the Greek Bible is Timothy Michael Law's *When God Spoke Greek: The Septuagint and the Making of the Christian Bible* (Oxford, 2013). Law's primary focus is the use of the Greek text of the Old Testament in the New Testament, and he supplies a wealth of information in this regard.

The best English translation of the Greek Old Testament is *A New English Translation of the Septuagint* (Oxford, 2007). This text was produced by the International Organization for Septuagint and Cognate Studies and published by the Society for Biblical Literature. It is valuable both for the quality of its translation and for the introductory notes for each book.

About the Author

THE V. REV. DR. STEPHEN DE YOUNG is the author of *God Is a Man of War* and *Religion of the Apostles* from Ancient Faith Publishing. He is the pastor of Archangel Gabriel Orthodox Church (Antiochian) in Lafayette, Louisiana, and holds a PhD in Biblical Studies from Amridge University. He hosts the *Whole Counsel of God* podcast and cohosts the *Lord of Spirits* podcast on Ancient Faith Radio. He is also the author of the *Whole Counsel* blog on the Ancient Faith Ministries website.

www.ingramcontent.com/pod-product-compliance
Lightning Source LLC
Chambersburg PA
CBHW031428120626
46545CB00006B/2312